MACMILLAN MASTER GUIDES

JULIUS CAESAR

BY WILLIAM SHAKESPEARE

DAVID ELLOWAY

with an introduction by
HAROLD BROOKS

M

MACMILLAN

First edition 1986

Published by
MACMILLAN EDUCATION LTD
Houndmills, Basingstoke, Hampshire RG21 2XS
and London
Companies and representatives
throughout the world

Typeset in Great Britain by
TecSet, Wallington, Surrey

Printed in Hong Kong

British Library Cataloguing in Publication Data
Elloway, David
Julius Caesar by William Shakespeare. —
(Macmillan master guides)
1. Shakespeare, William. Julius Caesar
I. Title
822.3'3   PR2808
ISBN 0-333-39768-1 Pbk
ISBN 0-333-39769-X Pbk export

Cover illustration: *Roman Art Lover* by Sir Lawrence Alma Tadema,
© Milwaukee Art Centre, Milwaukee, USA and by courtesy of Bridgeman
Art Library.

CONTENTS

GENERAL EDITOR'S PREFACE

The aim of the Macmillan Master Guides is to help you to appreciate the book you are studying by providing information about it and by suggesting ways of reading and thinking about it which will lead to a fuller understanding. The section on the writer's life and background has been designed to illustrate those aspects of the writer's life which have influenced the work, and to place it in its personal and literary context. The summaries and critical commentary are of special importance in that each brief summary of the action is followed by an examination of the significant critical points. The space which might have been given to repetitive explanatory notes has been devoted to a detailed analysis of the kind of passage which might confront you in an examination. Literary criticism is concerned with both the broader aspects of the work being studied and with its detail. The ideas which meet us in reading a great work of literature, and their relevance to us today, are an essential part of our study, and our Guides look at the thought of their subject in some detail. But just as essential is the craft with which the writer has constructed his work of art, and this may be considered under several technical headings – characterisation, language, style and stagecraft, for example.

The authors of these Guides are all teachers and writers of wide experience, and they have chosen to write about books they admire and know well in the belief that they can communicate their admiration to you. But you yourself must read and know intimately the book you are studying. No one can do that for you. You should see this book as a lamppost. Use it to shed light, not to lean against. If you know your text and know what it is saying about life, and how it says it, then you will enjoy it, and there is no better way of passing an examination in literature.

JAMES GIBSON

NOTE. References to the play use the line numbering of the Macmillan Shakespeare edition of *Julius Caesar* but, as all references are clearly identified, this Study Guide may be used with any edition of the play.

AN INTRODUCTION TO THE STUDY OF SHAKESPEARE'S PLAYS

A play as a work of art exists to the full only when performed. It must hold the audience's attention throughout the performance, and, unlike a novel, it can't be put down and taken up again. It is important to experience the play as if you are seeing it on the stage for the first time, and you should begin by reading it straight through. Shakespeare builds a play in dramatic units which divide into smaller subdivisions, or episodes, marked off by exits and entrances and lasting as long as the same actors are on stage.

The first unit provides the exposition which is designed to put the audience into the picture. In the second unit we see the forward movement of the play as one situation changes into another. The last unit in a tragedy or a tragical play will bring the catastrophe and in comedy - and some history plays - an unravelling of the complications, the *dénouement*.

The onward movement of the play from start to finish is its progressive structure. We see the chain of cause and effect (the plot) and the progressive revelation and development of character. The people, their characters and their motives drive the plot forward in a series of scenes which are carefully planned to give variety of pace and excitement. We notice fast-moving and slower-moving episodes, tension mounting and slackening, and alternative fear and hope for the characters we favour. Full-stage scenes, such as stately councils and processions or turbulent mobs, contrast with scenes of small groups or even single speakers. Each of the scenes presents a deed or event which changes the situation. In performance, entrances and exits and stage actions are physical facts, with more impact than on the page. That impact Shakespeare relied upon, and we must restore it by an effort of the imagination.

Shakespeare's language is just as diverse. Quickfire dialogue is followed by long speeches, and verse changes to prose. There is a wide range of speech - formal, colloquial, dialect, 'Mummerset' and the broken English of foreigners, for example. Songs, instrumental music, and the noise of battle, revelry and tempest, all extend the range of dramatic expression. The dramatic use of language is enhanced by skilful stagecraft, by costumes, by properties such as beds, swords and Yorick's skull, by such stage business as kneeling, embracing and giving money, and by use of such features of the stage structure as the balcony and the trapdoor.

By these means Shakespeare's people are brought vividly to life and cleverly individualised. But though they have much to tell us about human nature, we must never forget that they are characters in a play, not in real life. Remember, they exist to enact the play, not the play to portray *them*.

Shakespeare groups his characters so that they form a pattern, and it is useful to draw a diagram showing this. Sometimes a linking character has dealings with each group. The pattern of persons belongs to the symmetric structure of the play, and its dramatic unity is reinforced and enriched by a pattern of resemblances and contrasts; for instance, between characters, scenes, recurrent kinds of imagery, and words. It is not enough just to notice a feature that belongs to the symmetric structure, you should ask what its relevance is to the play as a whole and to the play's ideas.

These ideas and the dramatising of them in a central theme, or several related to each other, are a principal source of the dramatic unity. In order to see what themes are present and important, look, as before, for pattern. Observe the place in it of the leading character. In tragedy this will be the protagonist, in comedy heroes and heroines, together with those in conflict or contrast with them. In *Henry IV Part I*, Prince Hal is being educated for kingship and has a correct estimate of honour, while Falstaff despises honour, and Hotspur makes an idol of it. Pick out the episodes of great intensity as, for example, in *King Lear* where the theme of spiritual blindness is objectified in the blinding of Gloucester, and, similarly, note the emphases given by dramatic poetry as in Prospero's 'Our revels now are ended . . . ' or unforgettable utterances such as Lear's 'Is there any cause in Nature that makes these hard hearts?' Striking stage-pictures such as that of Hamlet behind the King at prayer will point to leading themes, as will all the parallels and recurrences, including those of phrase and imagery. See whether, in the play you are studying, themes known to be favourites with Shakespeare are prominent, themes such as those of order and disorder, relationships disrupted by mistakes about identity, and appearance and reality. The latter were bound to fascinate Shakespeare, whose theatrical art worked by means of illusions which pointed beyond the surface of actual life to underlying truths. In looking at themes beware of attempts to make the play fit some orthodoxy a critic believes in - Freudian perhaps, or Marxist, or dogmatic Christian theology - and remember that its ideas, though they often have a bearing on ours, are Elizabethan.

Some of Shakespeare's greatness lies in the good parts he wrote for the actors. In his demands upon them, and the opportunities he provided, he bore their professional skills in mind and made use of their physical prowess, relished by a public accustomed to judge fencing and wrestling as expertly as we today judge football and tennis. As a member of the professional group of players called the Chamberlain's Men he knew each actor he was writing for. To play his women he had highly trained boys. As paired heroines they were often contrasted, short with tall, for example, or one vivacious and enterprising, the other more conventionally feminine.

Richard Burbage, the company's leading man, was famous as a great tragic actor, and he took leading roles in seven of Shakespeare's *tragedies*. Though each of the seven has its own distinctiveness, we shall find at the centre of all of them a tragic protagonist possessing tragic greatness, not just one 'tragic flaw' but a tragic vulnerability. He will have a character which makes him unfit to cope with the tragic situations confronting him, so that his tragic errors bring down upon him tragic suffering and finally a tragic catastrophe. Normally, both the suffering and the catastrophe are far worse than he can be said to deserve, and others are engulfed in them who deserve such a fate less or not at all. Tragic terror is aroused in us because, though exceptional, he is sufficiently near to normal humankind for his fate to remind us of what can happen to human beings like ourselves, and because we see in it a combination of inexorable law and painful mystery. We recognise the principle of cause and effect where in a tragic world errors return upon those who make them, but we are also aware of the tragic disproportion between cause and effect. In a tragic world you may kick a stone and start an avalanche which will destroy you and others with you. Tragic pity is aroused in us by this disproportionate suffering, and also by all the kinds of suffering undergone by every character who has won our imaginative sympathy. Imaginative sympathy is wider than moral approval, and is felt even if suffering does seem a just and logical outcome. In addition to pity and terror we have a sense of tragic waste because catastrophe has affected so much that was great and fine. Yet we feel also a tragic exaltation. To our grief the men and women who represented those values have been destroyed, but the values themselves have been shown not to depend upon success, nor upon immunity from the worst of tragic suffering and disaster.

Comedies have been of two main kinds, or cross-bred from the two. In critical comedies the governing aim is to bring out the absurdity or irrationality of follies and abuses, and make us laugh at them. Shakespeare's comedies often do this, but most of them belong primarily to the other kind – romantic comedy. Part of the romantic appeal is to our liking for suspense; they are dramas of averted threat, beginning in trouble and ending in joy. They appeal to the romantic senses of adventure and of wonder, and to complain that they are improbable is silly because the improbability, the marvellousness, is part of the pleasure. They dramatise stories of romantic love, accompanied by love doctrine – ideas and ideals of love. But they are plays in two tones, they are comic as well as romantic. There is often something to laugh at even in the love stories of the nobility and gentry, and just as there is high comedy in such incidents as the cross-purposes of the young Athenians in the wood, and Rosalind as 'Ganymede' teasing Orlando, there is always broad comedy for characters of lower rank. Even where one of the sub-plots has no effect on the main plot, it may take up a topic from it and present it in a more comic way.

What is there in the play to make us laugh or smile? We can distinguish many kinds of comedy it may employ. *Language* can amuse by its wit, or by absurdity, as in Bottom's malapropisms. Feste's nonsense-phrases, so fatuously admired by Sir Andrew, are deliberate, while his catechising of

Olivia is clown-routine. Ass-headed Bottom embraced by the Fairy Queen is a *comic spectacle* combining costume and stage-business. His wanting to play every part is *comedy of character*. Phebe disdaining Silvius and in love with 'Ganymede', or Malvolio treating Olivia as though she had written him a love-letter is *comedy of situation*; the situation is laughably different from what Phebe or Malvolio supposes. A comic let-down or anticlimax can be devastating, as we see when Aragon, sure that he deserves Portia, chooses the silver casket only to find the portrait not of her but of a 'blinking idiot'. By *slapstick*, *caricature* or sheer *ridiculousness of situation*, comedy can be exaggerated into farce, which Shakespeare knows how to use on occasion. At the opposite extreme, before he averts the threat, he can carry it to the brink of tragedy, but always under control.

Dramatic irony is the result of a character or the audience anticipating an outcome which, comically or tragically, turns out very differently. Sometimes *we* foresee that it will. The speaker never foresees how ironical, looking back, the words or expectations will appear. When she says, 'A little water clears us of this deed' Lady Macbeth has no prevision of her sleep-walking words, 'Will these hands ne'er be clean?' There is irony in the way in which in all Shakespeare's tragic plays except *Richard II* comedy is found in the very heart of the tragedy. The Porter scene in *Macbeth* comes straight after Duncan's murder. In *Hamlet* and *Antony and Cleopatra* comic episodes lead into the catastrophe: the rustic Countryman brings Cleopatra the means of death, and the satirised Osric departs with Hamlet's assent to the fatal fencing match. The Porter, the Countryman and Osric are not mere 'comic relief', they contrast with the tragedy in a way that adds something to it, and affects our response.

A sense of the comic and the tragic is common ground between Shakespeare and his audience. Understandings shared with the audience are necessary to all drama. They include conventions, i.e. assumptions, contrary to what factual realism would demand, which the audience silently agrees to accept. It is, after all, by a convention, what Coleridge called a 'willing suspension of disbelief', that an actor is accepted as Hamlet. We should let a play teach us the conventions it depends on. Shakespeare's conventions allow him to take a good many liberties, and he never troubles about inconsistencies that wouldn't trouble an audience. What matters to the dramatist is the effect he creates. So long as we are responding as he would wish, Shakespeare would not care whether we could say by what means he has made us do so. But to appreciate his skill, and get a fuller understanding of his play, we have to distinguish these means, and find terms to describe them.

If you approach the Shakespare play you are studying bearing in mind what is said to you here, then you will respond to it more fully than before. Yet like all works of artistic genius, Shakespeare's can only be analysed so far. His drama and its poetry will always have about them something 'which into words no critic can digest'.

HAROLD BROOKS

1 LIFE AND BACKGROUND

1.1 LIFE

William Shakespeare was born in Stratford-upon-Avon in 1564. His father was a prosperous tradesman and occupied a number of important civic offices, but in the later 1570s his fortunes seem to have declined rapidly. In 1580 he was fined a considerable sum for some unknown offence and by 1592 he was failing to observe the legal requirement to attend church once a month for fear of being arrested for debt.

His son would almost certainly have been educated at the local grammar school, but there is no record of his early years until his marriage to Anne Hathaway in November 1582. It seems to have been a hasty marriage; a daughter, Susanna, was born six months later, followed by twins, Hamnet and Judith, in 1585. Within a few years of their birth Shakespeare had left Stratford for London. One can only speculate about the reasons for this move, but he must soon have begun his career as actor and dramatist; before leaving Stratford he could have made contact with the companies of actors that regularly visited the town, and his introduction to the literary world may have been helped by a Stratford friend, Richard Field, who had set up as a publisher in London. Shakespeare's earliest plays are generally dated 1589 or 1590 (his plays can rarely be dated with complete certainty) and by 1592 he was sufficiently well established for Robert Greene to warn his fellow university-educated dramatists against the competition from this upstart actor who presumed to write plays. By 1594 he was a member of the Lord Chamberlain's company, the most successful of the London theatre companies, which was led by the great tragic actor, Richard Burbage. They were frequently summoned to entertain the Queen, and when James I succeeded Elizabeth in 1603 they came under his personal patronage as the King's Men.

Shakespeare prospered in the theatre, becoming the most popular dramatist in the last decade of the century. He would have earned little as an actor or as a playwright, but he profited from sharing in the proceeds of the theatre itself; when the company moved to the newly built Globe

Theatre in 1599 he had a tenth share in the enterprise. Meanwhile he had acquired his own noble patron, the Earl of Southampton, to whom he dedicated his two narrative poems and may have addressed many of the sonnets he wrote during these years. By 1596 the fortunes of his family were sufficiently restored for it to be granted a coat of arms, and in 1597 he bought New Place, one of the largest houses in Stratford.

He remained a full member of the King's Men until at least 1611, the probable date of *The Tempest*, the last play that can be attributed wholly to him. He subsequently wrote a large part, if not all, of *Henry VIII*, but it is generally assumed that by then he was living in partial retirement. He died in 1616.

Shakespeare began by writing plays based on English history, ending with *Henry V* in 1599. In the same decade he wrote most of his comedies, but only two tragedies, although several of the history plays are tragic in form. *Henry V* was followed at the newly opened Globe Theatre by *Julius Caesar* (1599), the first of the great series of tragedies, which continued with *Hamlet* (1603), *Othello* (1604), *King Lear* (1605) and *Macbeth* (1606) and concluded with two more plays based on Roman history, *Antony and Cleopatra* (1607) and *Coriolanus* (1608), the former of which dramatises the later years of Mark Antony, when his infatuation with Cleopatra led to conflict with Octavius, his defeat and suicide. Shakespeare had not entirely given up comedy, but after *Twelfth Night* (1601) it lost much of its buoyancy and delight and, like the tragedies, explores the darker side of human nature. The 'dark' comedies – *All's Well that Ends Well* (1603) and *Measure for Measure* (1604) – are often linked with *Hamlet* and sometimes with *Julius Caesar* as 'problem plays'. They examine fundamental moral questions with an uncomfortably probing scepticism, and their comic resolutions at the end tend to raise as many problems as they solve.

1.2 JULIUS CAESAR AND THE HISTORY PLAYS

It is to the histories, however, that *Julius Caesar* is most obviously related by its political theme and by the sort of problem that it raises. There is the same fine balance of political and moral issues and the same awareness of the complexity and ambiguity of human motives. *Richard II* (1595) weighs the personal failings of Richard against his right as the legitimate king; the two parts of *Henry IV* (1596-8) set the fact that Henry is a usurper, with the murder of Richard on his conscience, against the need to maintain order in the kingdom. The rebellions that plague his reign are recognised as a punishment for his usurpation, but the rebels must nevertheless be defeated; even so, the rebel leader Hotspur is treated as sympathetically as the King's son, Prince Hal. Shakespeare's ability to sympathise with all types of men prevents any over-simplification, and one is constantly made aware of how political necessity may conflict with private morality. The relation of Hal with the old rogue Sir John Falstaff raises in an acute form the conflict between personal loyalties and the demands of public life that was to figure, if in quite different circumstances, in *Julius Caesar*, and their rival claims on our sympathies have aroused as much disagreement as have those of Caesar, Brutus and Antony. The witty and dissolute Falstaff symbolises the warmth and exuberance of human nature, but he also symbolises the disorder that threatens the country. While Hal amuses himself with him, he has always intended to reject him once he is king, as indeed he must do, but the rejection arouses regret and sympathy, and Falstaff is not forgotten even after Hal has become the hero-king, Henry V. The account of his death in *Henry V*, supposedly from a broken heart, is a superb fusion of comedy and pathos; and at the moment of Henry's triumph at Agincourt the King is compared to Alexander, not only for his military prowess but because both killed their best friends. A king cannot consort with characters such as Falstaff, but perhaps that shows the limitations of kingship: Henry must sacrifice much that is of value in human life to fulfil his political role - a theme that is equally prominent in *Julius Caesar*. Shakespeare presents the political and moral problems in all their complexity, but does not suggest any simple solutions, or, indeed, that any wholly satisfactory solutions are possible.

There are numerous references to Caesar in the histories, all of them complimentary, and Shakespeare clearly had him in mind as he was completing *Henry V*; when Henry returns from Agincourt the citizens of London

> Like to the senators of th' antique Rome,
> With the plebeians swarming at their heels,
> Go forth and fetch their conqu'ring Caesar in. (V. Chorus, 26-8)

But as Shakespeare turned his attention from English to Roman history his view of Caesar became much more complex, as is evident from a comparison of the above quotation with the attitudes expressed to Caesar's triumph in the first scene of *Julius Caesar*. This complexity is already found in the classical historians and biographers of Caesar, whose works Shakespeare had been reading, especially in Plutarch's *Lives of the Noble Grecians and Romans*, translated by Sir Thomas North in 1579, which was his principal source for the play.

1.3 THE HISTORICAL BACKGROUND

Rome was originally a monarchy, but towards the end of the 6th century BC the tyrannical Tarquinius Superbus was expelled, with Brutus's ancestor, Lucius Junius Brutus, taking a leading part in his expulsion. A republic was set up, governed by a senate composed of members of the noble families - the patricians - from whose ranks two consuls were elected annually by the whole people of Rome to exercise the powers formerly held by the king. Apart from voting for the consuls, the commoners – the plebeians – had little constitutional part in the government, although they were later allowed to elect two tribunes as their representatives. In times of crisis one man might be given absolute power as a 'dictator', a title that did not then have its present malign associations; he was appointed constitutionally and resigned when the crisis was over.

This constitution lasted for some five hundred years while Roman power was extended round the Mediterranean, but by the middle of the 1st century BC it was beginning to disintegrate. In 60BC Caesar, Pompey and Crassus formed the first triumvirate ('rule by three men') and governed Rome with little reference to the Senate. While Caesar was engaged in the conquest of Gaul, however, Pompey began to intrigue against him, posing as a champion of the Senate. Caesar invaded Italy, defeated Pompey at Pharsalus (48BC) and finally crushed all opposition with the defeat of Pompey's sons at Munda in 45BC, shortly before the action of the play begins. He was now supreme in Rome: in 45BC he was made consul for ten years and dictator for life. With his legions camped outside Rome, he already had the power of a king; all that remained was to establish a dynasty so that his position could be inherited by his descendants. As he had no legitimate children he made his grand-nephew, Octavius, his heir.

It is uncertain whether Caesar wished to become king. Plutarch thought that he did; like all the classical historians he admired Caesar's remarkable ability as a general, a politician, an orator and a writer, but considered his chief fault to be his ambition. His attitude to Caesar is ambivalent: he accuses him of hiding his cunning under an appearance of friendship, but denies that he was tyrannical, attributing the injustices committed under his rule to his associates and flatterers, notably Mark Antony. He praises, in particular, Caesar's clemency towards his defeated enemies who had supported Pompey, including Brutus and Cassius. He saved Brutus's life and made him a close friend; it was his appointment of Brutus as praetor – the officer responsible for the judiciary – instead of the more senior Cassius that made Cassius his inveterate enemy. Hence, while Plutarch had the highest opinion of Brutus, he blames him for ingratitude, and for failing to recognise that Rome could no longer be governed except by the absolute rule of one man: Caesar, in the words of North's translation,

> was a merciful Physician, whom God had ordained of special grace to be Governor of the Empire of Rome, and to set all things again at quiet stay, the which required the counsel and authority of an absolute Prince.

This opinion would have had a special appeal for Shakespeare's age, which, of course, did not share the Roman republican's distaste for kings. Legitimate monarchy was considered the ideal form of government, the mean between the opposite excesses of tyranny and democracy, but even tyranny was thought preferable to civil disorder, which was the worst of all political evils. Monarchy was upheld as the form of government ordained by God, the hierarchical order of king, lords and commons in the state reflecting the order of heaven and of the whole natural creation: as God is supreme in heaven, the king is supreme on earth. Yet such was the prestige of the Roman republic and its champions – men such as Cato, Portia's father, who committed suicide after the defeat of Pompey, or Cicero, who rallied the senate to oppose Antony after Brutus and Cassius had fled – that the most diverse estimates of Caesar and his assassins continued down to Shakespeare's day. Caesar might be seen as a tyrant who destroyed the greatness of the republic or as the ruler divinely appointed to prepare for the greatness of the Roman empire, which Octavius was to establish.

Evidence for both points of view can be found in Shakespeare's impartial treatment of the political situation in the play, and producers and critics have been almost as widely divided in their interpretations of *Julius Caesar* as the mediaeval and renaissance writers were of the historical Caesar. In 1937, for instance, Orson Welles presented Caesar, in modern dress, as a fascist dictator, while in 1957 Glen Byam Shaw's production at Stratford showed the 'northern star', to which Caesar compares himself (III.i.60), continuing to shine serenely over the defeat of his assassins as a symbol of the greatness that they could not extinguish.

2 SUMMARY AND CRITICAL COMMENTARY

Act I, Scene i

Summary

It is the Lupercal, the festival held on 15 February to honour Lupercus, god of flocks and herds, which Shakespeare combines with the triumph granted to Caesar in the previous October to celebrate his victory over Pompey's sons (see p. 4). The tribunes Marullus and Flavius rebuke a group of commoners for going to the triumph, and leave to do what they can to lessen the honours paid to Caesar by driving the crowds from the streets and removing the decorations from his statues.

Commentary

The play opens with a burst of lively activity as a care-free group of commoners in holiday attire crosses the stage and is suddenly checked by meeting the tribunes. Their mood is indicated by Flavius's description of them as 'idle creatures' and by the cheeky banter of the Second Citizen, to which his colleagues doubtless contribute with laughter and gestures as he avoids answering Marullus's questions with a string of puns. The audience is entertained by the neat word-play, especially beloved by the Elizabethans, and at the same time is being introduced to the situation at the beginning of the action, and to the underlying forces that will determine its course: the tension between Caesar and the former supporters of Pompey, and the irresponsibility of the Roman crowd, with its readiness to be swayed by powerful oratory. Marullus's speech (34–57) is the first of the great series of rhetorical speeches in the play, and is analysed in detail on pp. 75–7

The fickleness of the crowd is immediately evident: not only have they changed from cheering Pompey to cheering his conqueror, but they are soon persuaded to be ashamed of their new allegiance. As yet, though, there is no indication of the danger they present. This crowd is a group of cheerful individuals enjoying a holiday. The First Citizen is respectful of authority; the second welcomes the opportunity of mocking it, but it is all in good fun, and he is happy to joke against himself with his pun on 'cobbler', which could mean 'poor workman' as well as 'shoe-mender' (10-11). Marullus himself gives an agreeable impression of them (39-49) and both he and Flavius successfully appeal to their better natures (55-62).

Although representatives of the common people, the tribunes were often themselves patricians, hence their authoritative manner. Marullus is the more truculent; he is easily provoked and is either too indignant to see the Second Citizen's meaning or determined to get a straight answer out of him (10-19). Flavius is more conciliatory – he accepts the Citizen's indirect way of indicating his trade (21) and, while Marullus abuses them as 'blocks' and 'stones' (37), addresses them as 'good countrymen' (58) – but he too refers contemptuously to their 'basest mettle' (63) and proposes to 'drive away the vulgar from the streets' (72). There is no democratic feeling in Rome; the significance of the tribunes is as upholders of the rule of the patrician senate against the ambition of one man to seize absolute power. Flavius's final metaphor anticipates Brutus's speech at the beginning of Act II with its image of the un-hatched serpent (II.i. 10-34). It recognises both the greatness of Caesar – 'Who else would soar above the view of men' (76) – and the threat of this to the republic, but also implies that the threat is not yet realised, the feathers are only 'growing' (74).

Act I, Scene ii

Summary

Caesar enters in a ceremonial procession with the senators, accompanied by a great crowd. He reminds Antony to strike at Calpurnia during the race that was part of the festivities of the Lupercal as this was supposed to cure a woman of sterility. A Soothsayer warns him to beware the ides of March.

Alone with Brutus, Cassius sounds him on his attitude to Caesar. When the cheering in the forum surprises Brutus into revealing his fear that Caesar will be crowned, Cassius launches a bitter attack on Caesar, reminding Brutus of the part played by his ancestor in ridding Rome of tyranny. Brutus replies guardedly, but declares his unwillingness to live under the oppression that threatens them.

Caesar re-enters in an angry mood and, noticing Cassius, warns Antony of the danger he presents. As the procession leaves, Brutus detains Casca to tell them of the events in the forum: Antony had offered Caesar a coronet three times and Caesar's refusal had delighted the crowd, but in the midst of their acclamation Caesar had collapsed in an epileptic fit. He adds that Marullus and Flavius have been executed. Cassius arranges to meet Casca, and Brutus to meet Cassius, on the following day. Left alone, Cassius reflects on Brutus's character and resolves to send him letters supposedly written by various citizens urging him to defend Roman liberties.

Commentary

The political situation outlined in the previous scene is now presented concretely on the stage. The group of citizens who slunk away shamefaced is replaced by a great crowd acclaiming Caesar, showing the futility of the tribunes' attempts to stem this flood of hero-worship. The stage direction, '*after them Marullus and Flavius*', shows their detachment from these celebrations, and you should consider how they would be behaving; silent characters in a scene can still contribute significantly to the action.

The initial impression of Caesar seems to bear out their opinion. His first entrance in the play is designed to show his dominance. It may well be heralded by trumpets, which are needed later for the 'sennet' and 'flourishes' that accompany his triumphant progress (24, 78, 131). He walks, or is perhaps carried, in a ceremonial procession, attended by deferential senators, with even his wife and his best friend, Antony, keeping a respectful distance so that they have to be summoned to him when he wishes to address them (1, 4). His manner is autocratic, he gives curt orders and expects to be obeyed – as Antony says obsequiously, 'When Caesar says, "Do this," it is performed' (10). As soon as Caesar speaks, Casca is calling for silence (1, 14). It is significant that he always refers to himself in the third person, as 'Caesar' (17), as if he thinks of himself only in his public role. It is equivalent to the use of 'we' in proclamations by a monarch; even without a crown Caesar is behaving and speaking like a king. He shows no consideration for his wife's feelings when he refers in public to her sterility, and his wish that she be made fertile may reflect a desire to found a hereditary dynasty (see p.4).

The Soothsayer's voice – 'shriller than all the music' – pierces through the adulation. There is a dramatic hush as the triumphal music is silenced and he is brought to 'look upon Caesar'; while Caesar, although he may not know it, is brought face to face with his own fate in this brief interruption of the noisy celebrations of his triumph. The warning is uttered in all three times. Does Caesar brush it aside, or does he ponder it before dismissing the Soothsayer as a 'dreamer'? The man of action must at least pretend to despise such visionaries, but his concern that Antony should touch Calpurnia shows that he is not immune to superstition.

It is ironic that Brutus's first words in the play should be to warn Caesar of the assassination in which he will play the leading role (19); this is 'dramatic irony' – irony of which the speaker himself is unaware – and Brutus reports the Soothsayer's words with cool indifference. He maintains a similar detachment when left alone with Cassius, regarding the festivities in the forum with some contempt: 'gamesome' implies 'frivolous', and there is a note of self-satisfaction in his admission that he lacks

> some part
> Of that quick spirit that is in Antony. (28–9)

He takes leave of Cassius with aloof politeness, suggesting that Cassius may share Antony's superficial interests – 'Let me not hinder, Cassius, your desires'. Cassius clearly needs to be cautious, and he knows of the bond of affection between Brutus and Caesar (315); for the first part of their conversation he is carefully testing the ground. Brutus's coldness towards him gives him an opening (32-6), and he is reassured when Brutus reaffirms their friendship, if in somewhat restrained terms – 'Among which number, Cassius, be you one' – and, as a bonus, reveals his own troubled state of mind (39-47). We learn later that this inner conflict is between his love for Caesar and his fear that he will become king; and Cassius may suspect this, but instead of uttering his 'Thoughts of great value, worthy cogitations' (50) he shifts his approach with the sudden question, 'Tell me, good Brutus, can you see your face?', and continues to prepare the ground by telling Brutus in cautiously general terms of the hopes placed in him by 'many of the best respect in Rome . . . groaning underneath this age's yoke' (58-62). His caution is justified, for when he slips in an ironic suggestion that Caesar is assuming superhuman powers – 'except immortal Caesar' – Brutus is instantly alerted – 'Into what dangers would you lead me, Cassius . . . ?' – and backs away, disclaiming the 'worthiness' that Cassius has attributed to him. Cassius at once covers up; he feints by offering to be Brutus's 'glass' to show him the virtues he has denied, but in fact weaves away and seeks to allay Brutus's fears by emphasising his own trustworthiness. There is perhaps a subtle contrast between himself and Antony; his description of a superficially convivial but unreliable companion (72-8) accords with Brutus's slighting reference to Antony as 'gamesome' and with his later contemptuous account of him as given 'To sports, to wildness, and much company' (II.i.189).

So far Cassius has been circling his subject, trying various leads in order to find an opening. The opening comes with the shouts of the crowd from the forum. Brutus drops his guard and reveals his fear that Caesar will be king. Cassius leaps in:

Ay, do you fear it?
Then must I think you would not have it so; (80-1)

and Brutus admits the nature of the conflict within him: 'I would not, Cassius; yet I love him well'. He commits himself only in general terms, but his firm declaration that he will follow honour even at the risk of death emboldens Cassius to reveal his real object in an impassioned attack on Caesar.

The characters of the two could not be more sharply distinguished. While Brutus speaks of 'the general good' (85), Cassius reveals his personal hatred of Caesar. He picks up the word 'honour' but interprets it only in relation to himself, to his own status:

I had as lief not be as live to be
In awe of such a thing as I myself. (95-6)

This is not an ignoble sentiment, and he may have a genuine feeling for the equality of men, although he speaks of it again in personal terms:

> I was born free as Caesar, so were you;
> We both have fed as well, and we can both
> Endure the winter's cold as well as he. (97-9)

Brutus is included, but far from acting as a mirror to reveal Brutus's virtues, Cassius offers a highly dramatic account of his own. There is magnificent description of 'The troubled Tiber chafing with her shores' and of Cassius and Caesar 'stemming it with hearts of controversy', but it is Cassius who is the heroic figure – 'Accoutred as I was, I plunged in'; he even compares himself to Aeneas, the legendary founder of Rome (112). His eloquence is charged with bitter jealousy, heard in the contemptuous irony of 'the tired Caesar' (115), the sarcastic mock surprise of ''Tis true, this God did shake' (121), and the sneering 'As a sick girl' (128). He is clearly unfair to Caesar, both in his facts – for Caesar was a strong swimmer, and did not tell the Romans to 'write his speeches in their books' (126) – and his interpretations – most obviously when he attributes the pallor caused by fever to cowardice (122). Moreover, the mere fact that Caesar is subject to ordinary human ailments is not a reason for despising him; one might conclude instead that his achievements were the greater because he had to overcome physical handicaps. It is in fact Cassius who unintentionally provides one of the most splendid descriptions of the pre-eminence of Caesar in his indignant outburst,

> Why man, he doth bestride the narrow world
> Like a Colossus, and we petty men
> Walk under his huge legs, and peep about
> To find ourselves dishonourable graves. (135-8)

While he obviously exaggerates the abject state of the Romans, as he does earlier when he describes himself as 'a wretched creature' who

> must bend his body
> If Caesar carelessly but nod on him, (117-18)

the charge is given some substance by what we have already seen of Caesar's autocratic behaviour, and even Cassius's insistence on his physical disabilities has some relevance when set against Caesar's later arrogant claims to be more than human. One can sympathise with his exasperation at seeing a fellow human being assume so overbearing a manner.

One can also recognise the noble simplicity of Cassius's assertion of each man's personal responsibility for his lot,

> Men at some time are masters of their fates:
> The fault, dear Brutus, is not in our stars,
> But in ourselves, that we are underlings, (139-41)

as he turns from his own rivalry with Caesar to compare the names of 'Brutus' and 'Caesar'. Names are very important in this play; we have already seen the pride with which Caesar uses his (17). By comparing the two Cassius is opposing the republican tradition identified with the name of Brutus (158-61) to the domination of Rome by one man that 'Caesarism' represents. His passionate lament for the loss of the old republican breed – 'Rome, thou hast lost the breed of noble bloods' – is laced with bitter humour as he compares the physical qualities of the two names and puns elaborately on 'Rome' and 'room' (as 'Rome' was pronounced in Shakespeare's time). Finally he strikes at Brutus's most vulnerable point by invoking the name of the most celebrated of those 'noble bloods', his ancestor Junius Brutus, who expelled the Tarquin kings (see p.3).

Brutus must be moved by this appeal (see II.i.53-4), but he is probably influenced less by Cassius's malice against Caesar than by the ominous sounds from the forum. His reply again shows the difference between their characters. In contrast to Cassius's supple eloquence, with its dramatic examples, emotional outbursts and easy colloquialism – 'Ye gods, it doth amaze me . . . ' (128); 'Why man, . . . ' (135) – he offers a plain, scrupu-lously precise summary of the position he has reached, the orderly series of balanced statements reflecting his rational approach (162-5, 167-9). While Cassius flings himself into his cause, Brutus is almost pedantically circumspect and determined not to be rushed. He is prepared to discuss the matter further and his conclusion is resolute – something indeed for Cassius to 'chew upon' (171) – yet even here he discriminates, ignoring Cassius's extravagant descriptions of the servility imposed by Caesar and acknowledging only the latent threat of 'these hard conditions' (174).

The episode that follows provides a neatly compressed commentary on what has preceded it. Something has clearly gone wrong: Caesar is angry, Calpurnia pale, and the rest look like 'a chidden train' (183-5). Caesar certainly looks like a despot whose court must tremble when he is displeased. But if this helps to substantiate Cassius's accusations, Caesar, noticing Cassius standing apart with Brutus, unconsciously adds his own comment on the jealousy that prompted them:

> Such men as he be never at heart's ease
> Whiles they behold a greater than themselves. (208-9)

He gives a penetrating summary of Cassius's character, contrasting him with the convivial Antony (203-4) as Cassius may previously have con-trasted himself (72-8). He is 'a great observer' (202), as was apparent in his wary approach to Brutus, and Caesar catches precisely the sardonic humour with which Cassius has just been deriding him, and the thin-lipped smile with which he might have expressed his satisfaction at the limited effect of his 'weak words' on Brutus (175-7):

> Seldom he smiles, and smiles in such a sort
> As if he mocked himself, and scorned his spirit
> That could be moved to smile at any thing. (205-7)

This shows Caesar's shrewdness, but it is also the occasion for a further display of arrogance. Antony's reply, 'Fear him not Caesar', is careless both in dismissing the danger of Cassius and in tactlessly suggesting that Caesar might be afraid, and Caesar is stung into adding, 'Yet if my name were liable to fear'. Again there is the emphasis on his name; anyone with the name of Caesar must be incapable of fear, and his self-conscious insistence on this makes it no more convincing:

> I rather tell thee what is to be feared
> Than what I fear; for always I am Caesar. (211-12)

He claims to be above normal human failings, but immediately – as if to chime in with Cassius's contrast of Caesar's pretentions with his physical weaknesses – comes his reference to his deafness (213), an effect that must be deliberate as it is Shakespeare's own addition to the infirmities that Plutarch records of Caesar.

Casca's account of the events in the forum reveals a very different character from the sycophantic Casca at the beginning of the scene (1, 14). His 'sour fashion' (180) is the counterpart of Cassius's acid wit, but in place of Cassius's emotional rhetoric he affects a cynical indifference, as if such things were too contemptible for his notice: 'I can as well be hanged as tell the manner of it. It was mere foolery' (235-6). He speaks in blunt prose, and adopts a surly manner even with his friends, seeming reluctant to answer their questions – 'Why, you were with him, were you not?' (219); the constant prefacing of his answers with 'Why' suggests that the answer is so obvious that the question is not worth asking. Yet he has observed closely, even if the audience must allow for the bias in his interpretations. The offer of a crown may have been a device of Antony's to flatter Caesar – as Casca says, 'mere foolery' – or a way of testing the crowd's reaction, and Caesar was evidently angered by their demonstration that they did not want him to accept it. His displeasure may have been increased by the fear that he had marred his public image by fainting. Cassius is quick to seize on this further evidence of Caesar's physical weakness (252) and to turn it to his own purpose by pointing out that it is they who suffer from 'the falling-sickness' under Caesar's domination.

We see Caesar here as the demagogue, pandering to the crowd by continuing to refuse the crown even though their response angered him, showing his submission to them by offering his throat to be cut (265-7), and exploiting his swoon with the feigned humility with which he appealed to their sympathy (270-2); the theatricality of his performance is made explicit by Casca:

> If the tag-rag people did not clap him and hiss him, according as he pleased and displeased them, as they use to do the players in the theatre, I am no true man. (259-62)

Cicero also probably made an ironic comment on this performance, to judge from the way those who understood him smiled and shook their heads in a knowing, or rueful, manner (283-4); we know that he was indignant (185-8). He may have produced an apt Greek quotation, or spoken in Greek so that his critical remark would not be generally understood; Casca disclaims any knowledge of the language as if that, too, were beneath his notice.

The Roman commoners appear in a much less favourable light than they did in the first scene. We hear of them now not as individuals but as an undifferentiated crowd, easily swayed by a skilful demagogue and responding sentimentally to the emotion of the moment, so that it is unlikely that their enthusiasm at Caesar's refusal of the crown shows any real devotion to the republic. As Casca says of the wenches who 'forgave him with all their hearts',

if Caesar had stabbed their mothers, they would have done no less.
(275-6)

The events in the forum show how serious is the threat to the republic, with the crowd idolising Caesar and the suggestion made publicly that he should be crowned; and the conspiracy is unobtrusively moved forward. They help Brutus to make up his mind: previously he had asked Cassius not to press him further, but now it is he who proposes that they meet the following day (306-8), while Cassius prepares to recruit Casca by asking him to dine – Casca accepting in a typically churlish manner (290-4). Cassius's explanation that Casca is still 'quick mettle'

in execution
Of any bold or noble enterprise (299-300)

is further evidence of his insight, for it is Casca who strikes the first blow at Caesar.

Cassius is left to comment on Brutus's character with equal insight, but with a cynical realism that may be difficult to square with the apparently genuine regard he shows for him elsewhere in the play. He seems to be congratulating himself on his success in working on Brutus's 'honourable mettle' in spite of his nobility (310-12), implying that his own persuasion of Brutus has been anything but noble; 'noble minds' should not mix with cunning fellows like him (312-13). He even suggests that Brutus is foolish to sacrifice the advantages of Caesar's favour; the contrast between Caesar's attitude to himself and to Brutus clearly rankles with him, and he comments sardonically that if their positions were exchanged and Caesar loved Cassius as he now loves Brutus, Brutus would not be able to 'humour' (influence) him (315-17). Some critics have suggested, however, that 'He' in line 317 refers not to Brutus but to Caesar, so that Cassius is reflecting not on his success in influencing

Brutus but on the danger that Brutus will still be influenced by Caesar: having discovered that Brutus is open to persuasion (310-12), Cassius comments that men of noble mind should associate only with men of similar nobility, such as himself (312-13), and declares that even if Caesar loved him as much as he now loves Brutus, he (Caesar) would not be able to influence him (315-17). This interpretation is given some support by Plutarch's statement that Brutus 'might have been one of Caesar's greatest friends' but Cassius's friends 'prayed him to beware of Caesar's sweet enticements, and to fly his tyrannical favours'; but even if that were Shakespeare's original source for the speech, this reading of it is very strained. 'He' in line 317 refers grammatically to 'Cassius', which immediately precedes it, and the phrase 'and he were Cassius' would be both irrelevant and misleading if the second interpretation were intended. Lines 310-12 must refer to Cassius's persuasion of Brutus - 'yet I see' has the force of 'now I see' - and an audience could not know that Cassius's subject has changed from his own to Caesar's 'seduction' of Brutus. The former is the much more coherent interpretation, and if it seems uncharacteristic that Cassius should speak so cynically of the man for whom he elsewhere expresses such affection, one should note that he is quite unscrupulous in deceiving that man with forged letters (317-22).

Act I, Scene iii

Summary
Meeting Cicero, Casca describes the storm that is raging and the unnatural sights he has met with. Cicero regards them sceptically, but after he has left Cassius relates them to the unnatural political situation in Rome, and incites Casca into declaring his support for the conspiracy. Cinna enters and is sent to distribute more fabricated letters where Brutus will find them, before joining the other conspirators at Pompey's porch.

Commentary
The previous scene ended with Cassius's resolute couplet,

> And after this, let Caesar seat him sure,
> For we shake him, or worse days endure,

and the thunder and lightning underlines the threat. The entry of the terrified Casca, with drawn sword (19), conveys the fearfulness of the storm. He appears here in another unexpected guise as Shakespeare uses him to describe its fury and the unnaturalness of the prodigies that accompany it with vivid details: the tempest 'dropping fire', the slave whose hand flamed 'Like twenty torches joined', the lion that 'went surly by', the 'hundred ghastly women' 'drawn Upon a heap' (10, 15-23). He has been scared out of his cynicism into superstitious awe (54-6) and insists on the supernatural significance of these events in lines that directly contradict his earlier blunt realism:

> let not men say,
> 'These are their reasons, they are natural';
> For I believe they are portentous things
> Unto the climate that they point upon. (29-32)

It was, of course, common belief among both the Romans and the Elizabethans that there was a close relationship between the heavens, the natural world, and human society. Disturbances in the heavens would produce unnatural phenomena in the world of nature and political turmoil in the state, and, conversely, disorder in the state would be mirrored in the natural world and in the heavens. Casca envisages both possibilities: either the tumult on earth is a consequence of 'civil strife in heaven' (11) or men's insubordination has provoked the gods to stir up this tumult to destroy them (12-13). The intimate relationship between these different realms of existence is conveyed by the imagery, showing how this way of seeing the universe was ingrained in the imagination of the age: the 'sway of earth' ('sway' meaning 'government') links the natural world with the political state, and the disorder in the elements is seen as 'civil strife', with the 'ambitious ocean' rebelling against the natural order of things and striving to rise to the level of the 'threatn'ning clouds'.

The precise significance of the storm is left uncertain. The unnatural portents might reflect on the unnatural predominance of Caesar in a republic, or on the political upheaval planned by the conspirators. While an Elizabethan audience might have been expected to assume the latter (see pp. 4-5), it is striking that in this Roman context Shakespeare not only leaves the question open but emphasises this by Cicero's wise scepticism:

> But men may construe things, after their fashion,
> Clean from the purpose of the things themselves. (34-5)

His calm contrasts with Casca's panic. 'Why, saw you any thing more wonderful?' (14) is just the sort of question that the Casca of the previous scene might have asked, even to the deflating 'Why'.

Cassius, however, has no hesitation about interpreting these things 'after his fashion'. For him the storm is a fearful warning from heaven about the unnatural political situation in Rome; the state is 'monstrous' in the literal sense of a creature that is deformed (66-71). He draws an ironic comparison between the prodigies in the storm and Caesar's 'prodigious' behaviour (72-8), with the familiar contrast of Caesar's arrogance with his human limitations (76-7) and laments about the degeneracy of the Romans (80-4, 103-11; compare I.ii.150-7). The storm brings out his most theatrical manner. As the lightning 'seemed to open The breast of heaven', so he presented his own bosom 'Even in the aim and very flash of it' (48–52), identifying himself with the condemnation of tyranny that he pretends to see in the storm. But Cassius is an Epicurean (V.i.77–8), and the Epicureans were materialists who did not believe in portents, or that the gods interfered in human affairs, as he has already indicated (I.ii.140–1). He is posturing to inspire Casca with a similar resolution. When Casca tells him that the senate intends to offer Caesar a crown (85–8) he puts on a fine display of reckless determination to free himself from tyranny by suicide. It is another splendid passage of sustained rhetoric, rising to a climax through the repetition and balanced phrases (91–4) to exalt the freedom of the spirit over merely physical restraints. These may well be genuine feelings that Cassius is only heightening to impress Casca – after all, he does eventually commit suicide – although his pretence that he fears his grief has led him to betray himself to a 'willing bondman' (111–15) can only be a deliberate device. He clearly has no real doubts about Casca's loyalty when, indignant at being thought a 'fleering tell-tale', he affirms his support.

There is a mounting urgency throughout this scene. The storm conveys a sense of tumult and impending violence – it is

> like the work we have in hand,
> Most bloody, fiery, and most terrible (129–30)

– and the conspiracy has progressed from Cassius's cautious sounding of Brutus to a meeting of a committed group of conspirators, appropriately in Pompey's porch (121–6) – a porch of the theatre containing a statue of Caesar's old enemy. This rapid development is effected by Shakespeare's manipulation of our sense of time. At the beginning of the scene Cicero's question, 'brought you Caesar home?' suggests that it is still the night of the Lupercal, but at the end the conspirators leave to meet Brutus and at the beginning of the next scene we learn that this meeting is on the ides of March. Thus in the course of this scene we have moved from 15 February to 15 March, but an audience, swept along by the excitement of the storm, and of Cassius's rhetoric, is unlikely to notice this, especially as the meeting with Brutus would be vaguely associated with that arranged at the end of the previous scene.

The scene concludes with a series of rapid questions and instructions that also suggest mounting activity, and through it runs the fervent hope that they will gain Brutus's support (140–1, 153–64). Cassius claims that he is already three parts won – another indication of how far things have progressed – but takes the precaution of distributing more forged letters (142–6), while Casca makes clear why they value Brutus's virtues so highly:

> O, he sits high in all the people's hearts;
> And that which would appear offence in us,
> His countenance, like richest alchemy,
> Will change to virtue and to worthiness. (157–60)

Act II, Scene i

Summary
Early in the morning of the ides of March Brutus, in his orchard, considers how his decision that Caesar must be killed can be justified, a decision that is confirmed when Lucius brings him another of Cassius's letters. He describes his disturbed state of mind while Lucius goes to see who is knocking at the gate; learning that it is the conspirators with their faces concealed, he comments sadly on this need for deception. When the conspirators enter Brutus assumes the leadership and at once objects to the three suggestions that Cassius makes – that they swear an oath, enlist the support of Cicero, and kill Antony as well as Caesar. Decius reassures the others that he can persuade Caesar to come to the Senate in spite of the ominous portents, and Brutus undertakes to recruit Caius Ligarius.

When they have left Portia enters and eventually persuades Brutus to promise to tell her what is troubling him. The scene ends with Caius Ligarius declaring that the prospect of Brutus's leadership has cured his sickness.

Commentary
Brutus's opening words show that it is still night, and Shakespeare continually reminds the audience of this by the emphasis on the lighting of tapers (7-8, 35) and on Brutus's need for light by which to read the letter (44-5), by the two descriptions of the conspirators' arrival in the darkness (77-9, 276-8), and throughout the interchange between Brutus and Portia. Such scene painting was particularly necessary for the Elizabethan public theatre, where plays were presented in daylight, and it also serves a symbolic purpose. Cassius has already associated the conspiracy with the tempestuous night – it is 'A very pleasing night to honest men' (I.iii. 43, and see pp. 15-16) – and it is ominous that this final meeting of the conspirators, when they are joined by Brutus and complete the planning of the assassination, should be under the cover of a darkness that is associated both with 'evils' (79) and with sickness (235-6, 261-7).

The storm has now subsided, but there are still eerie lights in the sky – 'exhalations' are probably meteors, which were signs of ill-omen. Thunder rumbles threateningly as Brutus leaves with Ligarius (334), but at the beginning of the scene attention shifts from the political disorder in Rome to the psychological disorder in Brutus's mind, to which the vestiges of the storm provide a subdued background. The two are closely related; Brutus has already linked them when he described his inner conflict as a civil war (I.ii.46), and now he develops this comparison when he says that between the first promptings of a dreadful action and its execution,

> the state of man,
> Like to a little kingdom, suffers then
> The nature of an insurrection. (67-9)

The image derives from the renaissance view of man as a 'microcosm', or 'little world', a miniature replica of the universe – the 'macrocosm', or 'great world' – all the parts of which are reflected within the human constitution. Thus the political confusion in Rome is paralleled by the confusion in Brutus's mind, and both are mirrored in the tumult of the storm. As – for the Elizabethans – the king should rule in the state, so reason should rule over man's subordinate faculties; but in the condition that Brutus describes the 'genius' (normally a man's guardian spirit, but here probably meaning his soul or reason) and the 'mortal instruments' (his bodily faculties) are 'in council' (in debate) (66-7). His physical being is challenging the authority of his spiritual and rational powers. In effect, his reason or conscience has taken a decision, but he is recoiling physically and emotionally from it.

It is clear that Brutus has already taken the decision. The soliloquy at the beginning of the scene begins, 'It must be by his death' (10), and in what follows he is not debating whether or not Caesar should be killed but trying to justify this decision to himself. His motives are sharply distinguished from those of Cassius:

> for my part,
> I know no personal cause to spurn at him,
> But for the general. (10-12)

There is no doubt of Brutus's disinterestedness and concern for the general good, but the rest of this soliloquy suggests that rational principles and abstract morality may be as misleading as personal jealousy. His reasoning depends entirely on the fear of how Caesar might be changed by being crowned. He admits that there is no evidence that he would disjoin 'Remorse from power' (exercise his power without compassion) since he has never known Caesar to be controlled by his 'affections' (his personal desires) rather than by reason (18-21); it is characteristic that Brutus identifies morality with reason rather than with the 'affections'. He appeals instead to general experience ('common proof') that ambitious men pretend to be humble in order to climb to power but once they have achieved it they treat the subordinates who helped them to rise with contempt – 'So Caesar may' (24-7). Thus Caesar is to be killed because of what he might do, even though, according to Brutus, there is no indication of this in his past behaviour. He is condemned on a general maxim about human behaviour.

The comparisons with which Brutus attempts to justify this doubtful argument only accentuate its weaknesses. Caesar is twice compared to a serpent that is harmless in the egg but 'mischievous' when hatched by the warmth of the sun, the 'bright day' (14, 32-4), but Caesar is already enjoying the 'bright day' of popular esteem, and to refer to him in terms of an unhatched embryo, or 'young ambition' (22), is nonsense; he is already at the height of his career and it is unlikely that the addition of the title of king would produce such a change. The speciousness of the argument becomes increasingly apparent. Brutus admits that

> the quarrel
> Will bear no colour for the thing he is,

so he will

> Fashion it thus: that what he is, augmented,
> Would run to these and these extremities. (28–31)

'Fashion' has a disturbing suggestion of false contrivance, of twisting the argument, and he is unable to specify what 'extremities' would result. He again avoids the specific and thinks only in terms of general principles.

It is strange that Brutus ignores Caesar's autocratic behaviour, and even the treatment of Marullus and Flavius, but he seems uninterested in hard evidence. It is his abhorrence of the very idea of a king, the republican ideal for its own sake, and the duty he has inherited from his ancestors that are decisive:

> Shall Rome stand under one man's awe? What, Rome?
> My ancestors did from the streets of Rome
> The Tarquin drive, when he was called a king. (52–4)

It is this that inspires his final resolve:

> O Rome, I make theee promise,
> If the redress will follow, thou receivest
> Thy full petition at the hand of Brutus. (56–8)

This is a noble resolution, but it is ironic that it should be finally prompted by the deceitful letters sent by Cassius, and symbolically appropriate that Brutus should read them in the unnatural light of the ominous 'exhalations whizzing in the air' (44).

There can be no doubt that Brutus acts from a strong sense of duty. He so abhors tyranny that he is prepared to kill the man he loves to prevent even the possibility of its afflicting Rome, yet his profound unease about this decision is evident in his attempts to justify it as well as in his description of his disturbed state of mind. He is rationally persuaded that he should kill Caesar, but is instinctively recoiling from the deed. He can see it only as 'a dreadful thing' (63), and his honest, open nature is repelled by the underhand means that he must use. He is distressed even by the conspirators' elementary precaution of concealing their faces, and by the image of conspiracy it brings home to him; it has a 'monstrous visage' and he associates it with the 'evils' that are most free at night (77–81), although all he can substitute for physical concealment is a much more insidious hypocrisy, 'Hide it in smiles and affability' (82). His sense of duty appears all the stronger for the firmness with which he represses his repugnance, but this leads him into further illogicality and illusion throughout his meeting with the conspirators which follows.

To win the support of Brutus had been the chief object of Cassius and his colleagues, but when they enter Shakespeare does not dramatise their achievement. Instead he substitutes an unobtrusive symbolic comment on it. While Brutus tells Cassius privately of his decision the others fill in the time by discussing the direction of the east. This is often dismissed as incidental scene-painting, or as a realistic example of how men under stress discuss trivial things, but this talk of the sun rising must also reflect their impatience for the coming day and their hope that it will bring a new dawn for the republic now that Brutus is one of them. The 'high east' (110) – echoing their high hopes – is in the direction of the Capitol, where Caesar will be murdered, and Casca points towards it with his sword, which will strike the first blow.

They accept Brutus's leadership without question, and he assumes it with equal assurance, but the discussion that follows shows that the lofty idealism that makes him so valuable a figurehead results in a lack of realism that unfits him for the practical direction of the conspiracy. Cassius suggests reasonably that they swear an oath, but Brutus objects that this will debase the nobility of their cause, apparently assuming that they are all as trustworthy as he is, or at least determined to see them in that light. He expresses his own ideal with simple sincerity,

> what other oath
> Than honesty to honesty engaged,
> That this shall be, or we will fall for it? (126-8)

but he does tend to run on:

> Swear priests and cowards, and men cautelous,
> Old feeble carrions, and such suffering souls
> That welcome wrongs; unto bad causes swear
> Such creatures as men doubt ... (129-32)

Brutus may be carried away by moral fervour, or perhaps he welcomes the opportunity to demonstrate his own principles, or is even unconsciously reassuring himself as well as his listeners of the 'even virtue' of their enterprise (133). He certainly exaggerates the distressed condition of Rome by his confident appeal to

> the face of men,
> The sufferance of our souls, the time's abuse (114-15)

- rather as Cassius had done in I.ii. In marked contrast to the discriminating analysis he has just made in private of Caesar's potential for tyranny (10-34), he now implies that 'high-sighted tyranny' (118) already exists; 'high-sighted' suggests the soaring falcon seeking its prey with its sharp sight, recalling Flavius's comparison of Caesar to a bird of prey (I.i.74-7), but now Brutus speaks as if the 'growing feathers' were already mature.

The lack of realism in this extreme moral stance is immediately suggested by the discussion as to whether they should sound Cicero. The elevated view of the conspirators on which Brutus has just been expatiating contrasts sharply with Metellus's reference to their 'youths and wildness' (148) and with his argument that their immaturity will be concealed by Cicero's gravity; its calculating nature is emphasised by the imagery of bribery – Cicero's 'silver' hair will 'purchase' or 'buy' other men's approval (144-6). This, of course, is the very reason for their wanting Brutus to join them (see I.iii.157-60). But Brutus is oblivious of all this, as he is of the further irony that he should object to the inclusion of Cicero on the ground that

> he will never follow any thing
> That other men begin (151-2)

when he is displaying a similar assumption of the right to lead. To suggest this reflection on Brutus's behaviour Shakespeare alters the reason that Plutarch gives for Cicero's exclusion, which was his cowardice.

The others readily defer to Brutus's judgement; Casca, in particular, makes a striking *volte face* over Cicero, from 'Let us not leave him out' to 'Indeed he is not fit' (143, 153). Both these decisions could be serious errors: one of the conspirators must have talked for Artemidorus and Popilius to know of their plans (II.iii.1-10; III.i.13), and by rejecting Cicero they deprived themselves of the only man whose oratory might have countered that of Antony; but these are minor issues compared with Brutus's next intervention.

When Cassius, with his ability to look 'Quite through the deeds of men' (I.ii.203), recognises a 'shrewd contriver' in Antony and proposes that he be killed, we see Brutus at his best and his worst. His humane wish to avoid unnecessary bloodshed combines with his idealism: it is the spirit of Caesar (167) that they are opposing, the principle of absolute rule by one man and the Caesar-worship that is sweeping Rome. And since they cannot 'come by Caesar's spirit' without dismembering Caesar he tries to transform the assassination from a murder into a sacrifice – a sacrifice to the republican ideal:

> Let's carve him as a dish fit for the gods,
> Not hew him as a carcass fit for hounds. (173-4)

This is not necessarily unrealistic. There is sound political sense in not wishing to antagonise public opinion by appearing 'too bloody' (162) or malicious ('envious') (164, 178); but in trying to dissociate their action entirely from murder Brutus discounts the brutal physical reality of killing a man, and ironically it is Antony, for whose life he is arguing, who makes devastating use of this reality to destroy the conspirators. The imagery provides an unobtrusive comment on the degree of self-deception in Brutus's idealism. The analogy he draws between themselves and 'subtle masters' who

> Stir up their servants to an act of rage,
> And after seem to chide 'em (176-7)

is unfortunate, since the masters are deliberately deceitful, inciting their servants to an action from which the masters profit, but for which they can put the blame on the servants.

Moreover, behind Brutus's assurance that Antony

> can do no more than Caesar's arm
> When Caesar's head is off (182-3)

is a bland assumption of his own superiority. When Cassius persists in his opinion there is a disagreeable disdain in Brutus's reply that if Antony loves Caesar the most that can be expected of him is that he 'take thought' (take his death to heart) 'and die for Caesar'; and, he adds primly,

> that were much he should; for he is given
> To sports, to wildness, and much company. (188-9)

Cassius's protest is waved aside with equal condescension, 'Alas, good Cassius, do not think of him' (185); having worked so hard to gain Brutus's support Cassius must now watch him jeopardising the whole enterprise with his misplaced confidence that he knows best.

The final preparations further illustrate the moral dilemma in which Brutus is placed. There is more evidence of Caesar's weaknesses - his recently acquired superstition, from Cassius, and his susceptibility to flattery, from Decius - but Decius's malicious contempt for Caesar's gullibility and delight in his own cunning (202-11) are far removed from Brutus's idealised view of the conspiracy. Even so, he agrees to accompany the others to Caesar's house to second Decius (212-13) and himself offers to recruit Caius Ligarius, although Ligarius is motivated by hatred of Caesar, not noble patriotism. One might accuse Brutus of compromising his ideals, or with failing to see how unrealistic they are, but equally one might admire the resolution with which, having convinced himself of the right course of action, he goes through with it in spite of the distress it causes him. The dilemma is epitomised in his farewell to the others (224-7), when he urges them to show a similar 'constancy' by practising the deception that he abhors.

We move from Brutus wrestling to preserve his idealism amid the complexities of public affairs to the uncomplicated virtues of his private life - his sympathetic relationship with his wife and with his young servant Lucius, whom he considerately refrains from waking and whose 'honey-heavy dew of slumber' he contrasts sadly with his own sleeplessness:

> Thou hast no figures nor no fantasies
> Which busy care draws in the brains of men. (231-2)

Portia's quiet 'Brutus, my lord' startles him. He tries to avoid her questions by expressing concern that the night air is bad for her health, but she dismisses this with simple logic - 'Nor for yours neither' (237) - and is affectionately determined to find out what is disturbing him. As she steadily details all his irritable behaviour we gain a vivid picture of his troubled preoccupation and of her understanding and forbearance -

> Hoping it was but an effect of humour,
> Which sometimes hath his hour with every man. (250-1)

To his weak excuse that he is not well - the weaker in that he has just advised her to avoid the night air - she retorts with gentle irony,

> Brutus is wise, and were he not in health
> He would embrace the means to come by it, (258-9)

and when he replies impatiently she continues unperturbed, but with perceptibly sharper irony in the repetition of 'Is Brutus sick . . .'. One hears the humorous incredulity before she turns with affectionate intimacy - 'No, my Brutus' - to insist that the sickness is in his mind (268). Kneeling, she appeals more emotionally by the 'right and virtue' of her place as a wife, by her 'once commended beauty' - 'once' having the subdued suggestion that he no longer responds to it - and by their vows of love and marriage, 'Which did incorporate and make us one' (273); but through this moving appeal she reserves the one telling fact that she finally springs on him unobtrusively, as if it were part of her general inquiry:

> That you unfold to me, your self, your half,
> Why you are heavy, and what men tonight
> Have had resort to you. (274-6)

At this point Brutus must know that she has won. Now Portia insists more powerfully on her rights as a wife - 'your self, your half' - stressing the bond of marriage with a subtle play of legal terms - 'excepted', 'in sort', 'limitation' (281-3) - and asks if her role is only to satisfy his physical needs. If so, she dwells only 'in the suburbs' of his affection, 'suburbs' meaning 'outskirts', but as it was in the suburbs of London that the brothels were situated this leads to her conclusion, that she is then 'Brutus' harlot, not his wife' (287). This at last wrings from Brutus one of his few direct expressions of emotion:

> You are my true and honourable wife,
> As dear to me as are the ruddy drops
> That visit my sad heart; (288-90)

it is a tense statement, without lyricism, but the more powerful for having to break through the reserve he has hitherto maintained.

Until this last challenge to Brutus's love Portia has been gently persuasive, with a continual play of irony and innuendo; but now she asserts, and the change of tone is conveyed by the formal organisation of her speech, with its parallel statements linking the potent names of Brutus and Cato (see p.5) -

> I grant I am a woman; but withal
> A woman that Lord Brutus took to wife.
> I grant I am a woman; but withal
> A woman well-reputed, Cato's daughter (292-5)

- and her terse conclusion:

> Think you I am no stronger than my sex,
> Being so fathered, and so husbanded? (296-7)

As she had kept back her knowledge of Brutus's visitors until she could use it to greatest effect, so she has reserved for the climax of her persuasion the wound she has given herself as proof of her constancy (299-301), and Brutus is overwhelmed, his expression of love replaced by respect for her nobility (302-3). As he promises to tell her the secrets of his heart - 'All the charactery of my sad brows' (308) - his tone is melancholy and subdued; nowhere does one feel more strongly the weight of the sad duty he has imposed upon himself.

Although he is reserved in manner even with Portia, her knowledge of how to appeal to him, her subtle cajoling, the affectionate irony with which she exposes his excuses, even her precise observation of his irritated behaviour, show the closeness between them. She is the feminine equivalent of Brutus. Her earlier appeals to his love and her beauty are conventionally feminine, but her quiet assurance, the deftness with which she turns his words against himself, and her persistent calm reasonableness show her to be at least his equal in intelligence and strength of character. Moreover, she has a naturalness and warmth that contrasts with his austerity; there is no trace of that rather self-conscious posturing we may sometimes suspect in Brutus.

The entry of Caius Ligarius returns Brutus to the world of public affairs, and the scene ends on an optimistic note with Ligarius's ringing tribute:

> Soul of Rome!
> Brave son, derived from honourable loins,
> Thou like an exorcist hast conjured up
> My mortified spirit. (321-4)

Ligarius's casting off his sickness symbolises the renewal of health to the state of Rome, their enterprise 'will make sick men whole' (327); but there is also a sinister reminder that there are some whole that must be made sick. One might also feel a little uneasy at Ligarius's blind hero-worship, his readiness to follow Brutus 'To do I know not what' (333), while the miracle of healing symbolically attributed to him could even recall Cassius's charge against Caesar: 'this man Is now become a god' (I.ii.115- 16).

Act II, Scene ii

Summary
Disturbed by the storm and by Calpurnia crying out in her sleep, Caesar sends to the priests to discover whether the omens are favourable. Calpurnia enters, alarmed by the portents seen in the storm, and urges him to stay at home. Caesar dismisses both her fears and the advice of the priests, but when Calpurnia suggests that he inform the Senate that he is unwell he finally gives in to her. Decius enters and is instructed to tell the Senate that Caesar will not be attending its meeting, but Caesar refuses to send an untrue excuse, or to give any reason for his decision. He tells Decius, however, of Calpurnia's dream, and by reinterpreting this, and adding that the Senate intends to offer him a crown, Decius persuades him to change his mind. Caesar is further reassured by the entry of the other conspirators, whom he entertains hospitably.

Commentary
This scene is closely related to the two that precede it. The storm has returned and Calpurnia describes more portents of violence, to which are added the sacrifice of the augurers (38-40) - the Roman priests who foretold the future - and Calpurnia's dream of Caesar's statue running blood. As in I.iii, these portents are variously interpreted. Calpurnia voices the conventional view that they fortell the disruption of order in the state by the death of some great ruler. Her fears carry the more weight because she has formerly attached little significance to portents (13) and in spite of her agitation she speaks with authority:

> When beggars die, there are no comets seen;
> The heavens themselves blaze forth the deaths of princes. (30-1)

This would be the natural assumption for Shakespeare's audience, and even for a modern audience this accumulating of unnatural events builds up an impression of cosmic disorder as a background to the murder of Caesar.

The scene also develops those two characteristics of Caesar referred to by Cassius and Decius (II.i.193-211): his superstition - already suggested by his hope that Antony's touch can cure Calpurnia of sterility (I.ii.6-9) - and his susceptibility to flattery. But the most striking parallel with the previous scene is in the contrast between the portrayal of Caesar in his private life and that of Brutus.

In contrast to Portia's quiet approach Calpurnia enters in great agitation. She upbraids her husband, 'What mean you, Caesar?' - 'What are you thinking of!' - and actually orders him, 'You shall not stir out of your house today' (8-9). She has been frightened out of the submissiveness that she showed at her first appearance; perhaps she accepts this as her public role but is less submissive at home. However, this stridency is a sign of weakness rather than strength; she hasn't Portia's sympathetic insight into her husband. By sending to the augurers Caesar has shown that he too is concerned about the storm, but Calpurnia does not have the self-control to work patiently on this. Her tactless outburst only invites confrontation: 'Caesar shall forth' (10). It is remarkable that he continues to refer to himself as 'Caesar'; even when alone with his wife he needs to maintain his public image. His reply is arrogant,

> The things that threatened me
> Ne'er looked but on my back, (10-11)

but beneath the arrogance there are flashes of the real greatness of Caesar. There is genuine strength of character in his fatalism –

> What can be avoided
> Whose end is purposed by the mighty gods? (26-7)

– and in the objectivity of his comment that the portents 'Are to the world in general as to Caesar', and when Calpurnia counters this his reply shows the nobility of which he is still capable:

> Cowards die many times before their deaths;
> The valiant never taste of death but once. (32-3)

This has a memorable terseness, but he cannot leave it at that; he dwells on it self-indulgently, reducing its impact with an unconvincing expression of surprise that men should fear death, as if he were entirely immune to this common weakness. Similarly, when he hears that the augurers could not find a heart in the sacrificial beast, his interpretation of this as a reproof of cowardice is resolute (41-3), but as he dwells on the name 'Caesar' his boasting becomes absurd:

> Danger knows full well
> That Caesar is more dangerous than he (44-5)

is simply nonsense; 'Caesar' is elevated to the level of an abstract personification. Calpurnia's comment is shrewd: 'Your wisdom is consumed in
confidence' - he is eaten up with self-confidence.

Yet this extravagance probably reveals uneasiness in Caesar himself;
he is bolstering up his own resolution. When Calpurnia changes tack and
instead of trying to make him acknowledge the danger suggests that he
calls it her fear, and sends Antony with a message that he is unwell, he
readily accepts this way out, but as though he were merely indulging her
weakness: 'And for thy humour I will stay at home' (56).

With Decius present, however, Caesar is again in public view, and in
her anxiety Calpurnia makes a fatal mistake: 'Say he is sick' (65). But
Decius knows this is not true; 'Shall Caesar send a lie?' Caesar asks grandi-
loquently, although that is just what he has agreed in private to do! He
becomes still more dictatorial, insisting on his absolute authority with a
contempt for the 'greybeards' of the Senate that prevents one from
dismissing Cassius's accusations as mere envy:

> The cause is in my will; I will not come;
> That is enough to satisfy the Senate (71-2)

But this inflated image of himself is also a source of weakness. Decius's
technique is to alternate flattery, which blows up Caesar's self-esteem
still further, with mockery, which threatens to puncture it. He introduces
the latter with great care, suggesting only that he, not Caesar, might be
laughed at (69-70), although the reflection on Caesar himself is obvious
enough. There is just enough sting to make Caesar justify himself by
telling Decius of Calpurnia's dream, which he deftly reinterprets: the
smiling Romans bathing their hands in the blood gushing from Caesar's
statue are not rejoicing in his murder; it

> Signifies that from you great Rome shall suck
> Reviving blood. (87-8)

Decius's tone is smoothly reassuring:

> This dream is all amiss interpreted;
> It was a vision fair and fortunate, (83-4)

and Caesar purrs complacently, 'And this way have you well expounded
it' (91). Having added the bait of the crown, Decius can use the threat of

mockery more openly:

> Besides, it were a mock
> Apt to be rendered for some one to say,
> 'Break up the Senate till another time,
> When Caesar's wife shall meet with better dreams'. (96-9)

Caesar would seem dependent on the foolish whims of his wife; and, worse,

> shall they not whisper,
> 'Lo, Caesar is afraid'? (100-1)

By dramatising the Senate's response Decius makes Caesar hear the unthinkable sound of laughter behind his back while at the same time dissociating himself from any responsibility for the gibe, although he hastily protests that it is only his concern for Caesar's welfare that makes him venture so far. Caesar turns condescendingly to Calpurnia, who must be writhing in silent frustration,

> How foolish do your fears seem now, Calpurnia!
> I am ashamed I did yield to them, (105-6)

and is delighted to find so many senators coming to conduct him deferentially to the Capitol.

He greets each in turn, with a tactful word of condolence for his former enemy, Ligarius (111-13). Once again our sympathies fluctuate. Even here one might still sense the great man, mellowed by the promise of a crown, unbending to his subordinates, with perhaps a touch of condescension in his casual greetings – 'Now, Cinna; now, Metellus; what, Trebonius' – but he shows an ingenuous pleasure at their visit as he thanks them for their 'pains and courtesy', blames himself for being 'thus waited for' and invites his 'Good friends' to drink wine with him. It has been suggested that their drinking wine together is like a sacrament of friendship which the conspirators are about to desecrate. The word 'friends' is ironically stressed. Trebonius comments grimly,

> and so near will I be,
> That your best friends shall wish I had been further, (124-5)

and as Caesar prepares to go with them 'like friends' Brutus reflects sadly on the deception he has to practise:

> That every like is not the same, O Caesar,
> The heart of Brutus yearns to think upon. (128-9)

It is a last poignant insight into Brutus's troubled mind as he hardens himself to go to the Senate with his friend Caesar to murder him.

In the middle of this convivial meeting Antony enters, to see Caesar greeting each of his future murderers. It is a scene he remembers.

Cassius is absent. Knowing Caesar's mistrust of him he may have feared that his presence would alert his suspicions, yet it was he who proposed that 'all of us be there to fetch him' (II.i.212). A possible explanation is that in early productions of the play the actor who played Cassius, with a 'lean and hungry look' (I.ii.194), also played Ligarius, whose ague has made him lean (113). The two never appear together; Ligarius is unexpectedly absent from the assassination, but he must be present here as he left for Caesar's house with Brutus. This might also explain the unnecessary presence of Publius, who is not one of the conspirators (III.i.89–91); if Cassius had had to be omitted his name could easily have been substituted without disrupting the rhythm of the line (108).

Act II, Scene iii

Summary
Artemidorus stations himself on the way to the Capitol so that he can hand Caesar a paper warning him of the conspiracy.

Commentary
This and the next scene increase the tension as the moment of the assassination approaches by threatening to expose the conspiracy. Artemidorus's apparently disinterested esteem for Caesar helps to sway our sympathies in his direction: he is identified with 'virtue', and the conspirators with 'emulation' (envy) (13–14). At the same time he warns Caesar of the weakness that will expose him to their daggers: 'Security gives way to conspiracy' (7–8) – a false sense of security opens the way for conspiracy to achieve its aim – echoes Calpurnia's 'Your wisdom is consumed in confidence' (II.ii.49); and 'If thou beest not immortal, look about you' is advice that Caesar might well heed when he identifies himself with the immortal gods immediately before he is murdered (III.i.74).

Act II, Scene iv

Summary
Portia enters in great agitation and attempts three times to send Lucius to the Senate before she can think of any reason for his going. The Soothsayer tells her that he has a petition for Caesar that concerns Caesar's own welfare.

Commentary
The anxiety of Artemidorus for Caesar is balanced by that of Portia for

Brutus, and the tension is further raised by her agitation and by the fear that she may inadvertently disclose the plot, which Brutus has evidently disclosed to her. Her distraction seems to belie her claim to be superior to her sex, when she displayed the strong proof of her constancy (II.i.296-301). Now she appeals desperately to 'constancy' and confesses, 'I have a man's mind, but a woman's might' (6-8). Twice she chides Lucius for not having gone to the Senate, although she hasn't told him what he is to do there (3, 10); she is alarmed by any noise, thinking she hears an outcry in the Capitol, a 'bustling rumour, like a fray' (18), although Lucius has heard nothing; and she blurts out her concern for Brutus's 'enterprise' within Lucius's hearing and hastily tries to cover her indiscretion by adding unconvincingly, 'Brutus hath a suit That Caesar will not grant' (42-3) - if the enterprise were so innocuous there would be no need for the explanation!

Portia laments 'how weak a thing The heart of woman is' (39-40), but the real reason for her agitation is that she can do nothing, only wait. All she wants is to be with Brutus and she sends Lucius to the Senate simply as a means of contact with him; she hastily invents a reason - that Brutus is unwell - and, collecting her thoughts, tells Lucius to observe what happens there (13-15), but she has forgotten about this by the end of the scene, when she merely sends Brutus her love, reassures him that she is in good spirits, and tells Lucius to return with Brutus's reply (44-6).

The reappearance of the Soothsayer can only increase Portia's alarm; she heard his original warning to Caesar. She questions him urgently, guesses his intention (27), and when he tells her his petition is to beg Caesar to look to his own safety, 'to befriend himself', she tries anxiously to discover how much he knows (31).

Like Artemidorus, the Soothsayer moves off in the direction of the Capitol, the focus of the tragedy, and time moves inexorably on: at the end of II.ii. Brutus confirmed that it was 8 o'clock; now it is 'About the ninth hour' (23).

Act III, Scene i

Summary

The crowd gathers outside the Senate House, which is open to the street so that events inside can be seen. Caesar enters with the senators, commenting ironically to the Soothsayer that the ides of March have come, but the Soothsayer replies that they have not yet gone. Artemidorus tries in vain to persuade Caesar to read his petition. Cassius is alarmed when Popilius Lena reveals that he knows of the plot, but Brutus reassures him. Trebonius draws Antony out of the way and the others gather round Caesar under the pretence of supporting Metellus Cimber's petition. Caesar refuses to consider it and is insisting that his decisions are immutable when Casca stabs him from behind, followed by the other conspirators. Seeing that Brutus is one of his murderers Caesar resigns himself to death.

The crowd and the other senators disperse in alarm, leaving the conspirators to celebrate their achievement. Antony sends a conciliatory message and after Brutus has guaranteed his safety deceives him into thinking he will join with them; in spite of Cassius' objections he is allowed to speak at Caesar's funeral. Left alone, Antony vows vengeance and prophesies blood and destruction throughout Italy. A servant reports that Octavius is approaching and Antony decides to test the mood of the people with his funeral oration before deciding whether it is safe for him to enter Rome.

Commentary
Caesar enters ceremonially, announced by a trumpet fanfare, and closely attended by the conspirators. He has remembered the Soothsayer's warning, even though he pretended to dismiss it at the time, but his comment that 'The ides of March are come' - yet nothing untoward has happened - suggests that his earlier fears are entirely set at rest. The Soothsayer contents himself with the equally laconic reply, 'Ay, Caesar, but not gone' - there is still time for his forebodings to be realised. It is a terse and pregnant opening to the scene.

The tension rises with Artemidorus's desperate attempts to persuade Caesar to read his schedule, while the conspirators try to distract Caesar's attention. But, like Calpurnia (II.ii.65), in his anxiety Artemidorus makes the mistake of urging Caesar to behave in a way that would mar his public reputation, and Caesar responds with the sort of gesture that would be expected of him: 'What touches us ourself shall be last served' (8). Yet it is a magnanimous reply, even if one suspects Caesar's motives in making it, and might even recall Brutus's admission that he had never known Caesar to be moved by his personal desires rather than by reason (II.i. 20-1).

The suspense is further increased by Popilius's remark that he hopes their enterprise may thrive and his cryptic refusal to say more. Cassius nearly panics; it is unexpected that he should turn to Brutus for practical advice in a crisis, asking helplessly, 'What shall be done?', but while he lapses into his favourite dramatic gesture, it is Brutus who keeps control of the situation, watching Caesar's response to Popilius, and showing the 'formal constancy' that he had recommended to the others (II.i.227) and with which he now fortifies Cassius: 'Cassius, be constant'.

The plan now develops smoothly as Trebonius distracts Antony's attention and the others 'press near' to support Metellus. Caesar turns magnificently:

> What is now amiss
> That Caesar and his senate must redress? (31-2)

As ever, he is 'Caesar' and it is 'his' senate; he speaks as if it were merely an instrument of his will (see II.ii.71-2). Again we see him degenerate from the expression of sentiments noble in themselves through a self-satisfied dwelling on them, to an arrogance that is absurd in its extravagance. He very properly rebukes Metellus for supposing that his exaggerated humility could influence the course of justice, treating fundamental law – 'pre-ordinance and first decree' (38) – as if it were a childish game; but what he stresses is that he, Caesar, is not like 'ordinary men' who might be stirred by such humility, and he develops this through a complex statement that associates flattery with melting sweetness – 'thawed', 'melteth', 'sweet words' – and fawning dogs – 'base spaniel fawning', 'like a cur' (39–46). Considerable speculation has been aroused about the conclusion of this speech by Ben Jonson's statement in *Discoveries* (1640) that Shakespeare had been ridiculed for making Caesar say, 'Caesar did never wrong but with just cause'. As Jonson quotes it the line does not appear in any edition of the play, so it is possible that the ridicule led to the substitution of the printed version,

> Know, Caesar doth not wrong, not without cause
> Will he be satisifed;

replacing an apparent contradiction with something innocuous, if rather pointless. John Palmer, however, defends the line as Jonson quotes it as the culmination of Caesar's arrogance: 'It is the last . . . assumption of the man who lives for power that the wrong he does is right'. One might go further and question whether the statement is as malign as Palmer suggests. It could mean only that the end must sometimes justify the means, that it may be necessary to wrong an individual for the sake of the general good. One may not approve, but politics often demands such rough justice – indeed, is not Brutus doing 'wrong' to Caesar by killing him for what he *might* do in order to uphold the 'just cause' of republicanism? The only surprising thing is that Caesar is prepared to state this openly.

The renewed pleas of Metellus, supported by Brutus, who carefully distinguishes his gesture of respect from flattery, and Cassius, who has no such compunction, encourage Caesar to an even more egotistical flight. Enlarging on his superiority to other men, he first compares himself to the physical heavens – to the pole star which alone is motionless in the sky (60–2) – and then, as the appeals of the conspirators become shorter and more rapid, he overwhelms them by identifying himself with the whole pantheon of Roman gods:

> Hence! wilt thou lift up Olympus? (74)

– at which point Casca strikes, cutting through the rhetoric with his terse, 'Speak hands for me!' He will speak with his actions, not words.

The murder of Caesar is a highly dramatic event in itself as the conspirators press round the solitary figure trying to avoid their daggers, for he must not die at once so that each of them can play his part in the killing, until Brutus delivers the final blow and he falls, significantly at the foot of Pompey's statue (see pp. 43–4). But it is made still more dramatic by being the focus of two of the major themes in the play. The first is the continual contrasting of Caesar's claim to be more than human with the evidence of his all too human weaknesses. There is obvious irony in this final demonstration of his human vulnerability coming at the moment when his arrogance has reached a peak, when he is claiming to be 'constant', 'true-fixed', 'unassailable' and 'Unshaked of motion', and comparing himself to the Olympian gods. But there is another side of Caesar's humanity which flashes out at the moment of his death in the words 'Et tu, Brute?' – implying 'Even you as well, Brutus?'. If Brutus stabs him he will no longer resist: 'Then fall, Caesar!' This is the Caesar who is capable of human affection and of inspiring affection. We glimpse it in his genial hospitality when the conspirators come to conduct him to the Senate, but for the most part we have to recognise Caesar's love for Brutus from its reflection in the love of Brutus for Caesar.

This most emphatic expression of Caesar's humanity is inseparable from the second theme that reaches its climax at the murder, the conflict between Brutus's love for Caesar and his duty to the republic. Shakespeare has unobtrusively reminded us of it immediately before the murder, in Caesar's surprise that Brutus should support Metellus – 'What, Brutus?' (55) – and in his last words before Casca strikes, 'Doth not Brutus bootless kneel?' – even the greatly loved Brutus cannot move him. It is a most poignant moment: just when Brutus is sternly demonstrating the triumph of duty over love by thrusting his dagger into Caesar, Caesar demonstrates his love of Brutus by ceasing to resist the dagger thrusts. Momentarily he stops thinking of himself and thinks of Brutus; although one must also note that he still dies, magnificently, in the third person: 'Then fall, Caesar'. Even so, there must be a surge of sympathy for Caesar as we suddenly see a side of his nature of which for the most part we have only been told instead of experiencing it directly.

There is no indication whether Brutus is aware of this. He acknowledges only the potential tyrant in Caesar when he tells the frightened onlookers 'Ambition's debt is paid' (83), and seems caught up in the general euphoria. The effect of what follows is ambiguous. This is the moment of triumph; Cinna proclaims 'Liberty! Freedom! Tyranny is dead!' – but his words fall hollowly in the rapidly emptying Senate. Amid the general confusion (96–8) the conspirators seem equally confused. They have made no plans and give contradictory advice. Cinna and Cassius urge that they disperse to proclaim the news through Rome, but Metellus advises that they 'Stand fast together' lest they be attacked. They seem not to have considered the possibility, and it is not considered now; Brutus cuts Metellus off in midsentence (89), although Cassius now seems to agree with him (92–3).

Instead of consolidating their position they indulge in empty heroics, and, surprisingly, it is the sober Brutus who takes the lead, flinging out a superficially impressive truism about fate: we know we shall die, all we want to know is when we shall die (98-100). Casca takes this up with what would seem to be a cynical comment – by shortening a man's life one merely reduces the period for which he would have been fearing death – but even more remarkably, Brutus endorses this, 'So are we Caesar's friends'. Can he be trying to persuade himself, with staggering philosophical objectivity, that they have actually done Caesar a favour? The thought recalls Caesar's own words,

> Cowards die many times before their deaths;
> The valiant never taste of death but once (II.ii.32-3)

but it is one thing to contemplate one's own death with such a reflection and quite another to make it about the death of a friend whom one has just stabbed!

Brutus's next move is more characteristic. He had previously represented the assassination as a sacrifice (II.i.166, 173), and now he proposes that they bathe their arms in Caesar's blood, 'Up to the elbows', as a solemn ritual gesture to show that they are 'sacrificers' and not 'butchers'. His words have a ceremonial movement, 'Stoop Romans, stoop', but he fails to see that their bloody hands can only draw attention to the physical brutality of the murder, and the irony of crying 'Peace' while waving their blood-stained weapons (109-10) escapes him entirely. The gesture appeals to Cassius's dramatic instincts, and its theatrical nature is emphasised when he and Brutus anticipate how their deed will be presented by actors through succeeding ages. Again Shakespeare preserves a balance: they may be indulging in self-dramatisation, but he is using the presentation of his own play in the Globe Theatre as concrete evidence of the lasting fame they have achieved, so that their 'lofty scene' is

> acted over
> In states unborn, and accents yet unknown. (112-3)

In contrast to their heady mood, the entry of Antony's servant introduces a new voice into the play, supple and assured. We have seen little of Antony, but from the first words of his servant, whose careful phrases show that he is reproducing precisely what Antony has told him to say, the tone is unmistakeable. Antony is testing the ground, and carefully balances praise of Caesar with praise of Brutus, although he subtly adds 'feared' to Caesar (126-9). He would be foolish to try to deny his love for Caesar, but there is now a plausible distinction to be made:

> Mark Antony shall not love Caesar dead
> So well as Brutus living. (133-4)

All he asks is that Brutus will guarantee his safety and explain why Caesar had to die. Brutus obviously cannot refuse, but his complacency is frightening: 'I know that we shall have him well to friend' (143). Cassius is uneasy, and, as he rightly says, his

> misgiving still
> Falls shrewdly to the purpose. (145-6)

From his entrance Antony seems in complete control of the situation, cooly ignoring Brutus's welcome and addressing the body of Caesar. As he recalls his 'conquests, glories, triumphs, spoils' (149) the audience, and the conspirators, are being reminded of the genuine greatness of Caesar; now that he is dead the extravagant posturing that we have seen is being forgotten and the legendary Caesar of whom we have heard is being recreated. Then Antony turns to the conspirators and with splendidly careless gallantry offers them his own life:

> If I myself, there is no hour so fit
> As Caesar's death hour, nor no instrument
> Of half that worth as those your swords, made rich
> With the most noble blood of all this world. (153-6)

Throughout this encounter he combines praise of Caesar and savage references to the brutality of his murder with extravagant respect for the assassins. Their 'purpled hands do reek and smoke' (158), but they are 'The choice and master spirits of this age' (163). While venting his feelings about the murder he gives the impression of guileless honesty in the open expression of his grief. In this he can be entirely sincere, there is genuinely intimate affection when he addresses Caesar by his personal name, 'Pardon me, Julius' (204) – the first time it is used in the play – and refers to himself as 'thy Antony' (197), but at the same time he is using it to impose on Brutus. He knows, of course, that he is perfectly safe in offering his life to him. Brutus would not think of consenting to his death after such a demonstration of loyalty to a dead friend. It was after all Brutus who said,

> If he love Caesar, all that he can do
> Is to himself, take thought, and die for Caesar, (II.i.186-7)

and if he remembers now the contemptuous tone in which he said it he may even be feeling a little ashamed.

Brutus is clearly moved and almost pleads with him, 'O Antony, beg not your death of us', assuring him that it is only pity for Rome that has driven out pity for Caesar:

> Though now we must appear bloody and cruel,
> As by our hands and this our present act
> You see we do. (165-7)

So much for his attempt to show the sacrificial nature of the murder by bathing their hands in Caesar's blood! Through the rest of the scene we watch the exposure of all Brutus's idealistic illusions about the assassination.

Cassius tries to counter the political innocence of Brutus's open-hearted offer of friendship to Antony (172-6) with his own political realism by offering him a share in the spoils (177-8), but Antony ignores this and plays along with Brutus as he enacts his own ironic ritual. He takes each of them by the 'bloody hand' to seal his pretended friendship with them, while in fact marking each down for vengeance – with a special word for 'my valiant Casca', who struck Caesar from behind, and 'good Trebonius', who had prevented Antony from intervening in the murder. The audience may recall how Brutus had taken these same hands 'all over, one by one' in such good faith that he rejected any oath other 'Than honesty to honesty engaged' (II.i.112, 127), but Antony remembers how Caesar had greeted each in turn that morning, and now matches the conspirators' duplicity with his own. He takes a savage delight in the pantomime, relishing the irony in the pause that follows 'Gentlemen all' (190).

He turns again to address the dead Caesar, with the first unobtrusive reference to Caesar's spirit (195) that will be so powerful a force through the rest of the play, and even as he flatters the conspirators by comparing him to 'a deer, strucken by many princes' another of Brutus's illusions is exposed. Brutus had wanted to carve Caesar

> as a dish fit for the gods,
> Not hew him as a carcass fit for hounds, (II.i.173-4)

but now the

> hunters stand,
> Signed in thy spoil, and crimsoned in thy lethe. (205-6)

'Spoil' is a hunting term for the division of the quarry among the hounds, and it is as 'hunters' that the conspirators are 'crimsoned' by Caesar's death and indelibly marked, 'signed', with his blood. To Brutus's idealistic theories Antony opposes the plain physical facts. Brutus had wanted to 'come by Caesar's spirit, And not dismember Caesar' (II.i.169-70); Antony focuses attention on the dismembering, the bloody evidence of which is all too apparent thanks to Brutus's ritual action. It seems that that is all Brutus has achieved, while Caesar's spirit is being revived by Antony's evocation of his greatness, a greatness which the conspirators cannot deny; when Cassius interrupts uneasily Antony can give the bland reply,

> Pardon me, Caius Cassius,
> The enemies of Caesar shall say this;
> Then, in a friend, it is cold modesty. (211-13)

Cassius comes bluntly to the point, 'Will you be pricked in number of our friends ... ?' and Antony replies with equal suavity, 'Therefore I took your hands', casually dropping in another word that will become charged with meaning,

> Upon this hope, that you shall give me reasons
> Why, and wherein, Caesar was dangerous. (221-2)

Brutus picks it up readily; their 'reasons are so full of good regard' that even if Antony were the son of Caesar he would be satisfied. Antony has one more small request, which he makes as if it were a matter of course, that he be allowed to produce Caesar's body and speak at his funeral 'as becomes a friend' (229). When Brutus agrees Cassius makes his strongest protest, telling him bluntly, 'You know not what you do', but Brutus waves him aside with the same polite condescension he had shown in his orchard:

> By your pardon;
> I will myself into the pulpit first,
> And show the reason of our Caesar's death. (235-7)

He has sublime confidence in his own powers of persuasion and of the crowd's readiness to be convinced by 'reason'. He argues sensibly that it will be to their advantage to give Caesar 'all true rites and lawful cere-monies' (241), but he totally underestimates Antony, who has emerged as a man after his own heart by his display of loyalty to Caesar and his readiness, nevertheless, to listen to 'reasons'. He happily associates himself with him in the phrase 'our Caesar's death' (237) and proceeds with calm assurance to set out their conditions (245-51). Antony's humble acquies-cence is loaded with irony: 'Be it so; I do desire no more' (251-2). He doesn't need any more.

Left alone, Antony rends Brutus's view of the assassination into tatters. The conspirators are now explicitly 'butchers' (255); Caesar's wounds

> like dumb mouths do ope their ruby lips,
> To beg the voice and utterance of my tongue, (260-1)

and in the next scene Antony will give them a voice as he displays them to the crowd. Caesar has become

> the ruins of the noblest man
> That ever lived in the tide of times, (256-7)

and so far from 'coming by' Caesar's spirit Brutus has merely succeeded in turning it into a terrifying spirit of revenge (270 and, with supreme irony, giving it 'a monarch's voice' (272). In trying to prevent Caesar becoming king he has unleashed a far greater tyranny, with Caesar associated now not with the Olympian gods (74) but with Ate, goddess of discord (271). Sympathy with Antony's grief and admiration for his courage and subtlety are now qualified by his lust for revenge, which will 'cumber all the parts of Italy'; one cannot miss the relish in his savage prophecy (262-75).

Yet Antony remains self-controlled through the strongest emotion. With the entry of Octavius's servant he turns at once to practical affairs, and although the servant's sudden tears at the sight of Caesar's corpse reawaken his own grief that does not divert him from the business in hand. First he decides that Rome is too dangerous for the young Octavius, but, thinking quickly, he resolves first to test the reaction of the people with his funeral oration. Antony is always an opportunist, ready to exploit the opportunities that the immediate moment offers.

Act III, Scene ii

Summary

Brutus addresses the crowd in the forum and wins their support, but Antony subtly turns them against the conspirators and they rush off to kill them and burn their houses. A servant informs Antony that Octavius has arrived in Rome and that Brutus and Cassius have fled.

Commentary

The crowd is restless, demanding to be 'satisfied' that Caesar's death was merited, but still capable of sensible judgements: one of them suggests that they compare what Brutus and Cassius say to check that they agree in their explanations (9-10).

Plutarch does not record the content of Brutus's speech, but he says his style imitated 'the brief, compendious manner of the Lacedaemonians' (the Lacedaemonians, or Spartans, inhabited Laconia, from which we derive the term 'laconic'). Shakespeare clearly modelled the speech on this. It is both brief and 'compendious' - packed with meaning - a concentration that is achieved by the closely knit series of parallel statements; clauses having the same structure are balanced against each other - often antithetically, with the second of a pair of statements being opposite in meaning to the first. It is identical to the style that Plutarch illustrates by a letter from Brutus to the Pergamenians,

I understand you have given Dolabella money: if you have done it willingly, you confess you have offended me; if against your wills, show it then by giving me willingly,

and another to the Samians, 'Your councils be long, your doings be slow, consider the end'.

Brutus speaks in prose, as befits the plain appeal to reason that he purports to make, but it is the complex prose of a scholar, skilled in rhetorical devices. He weaves intricate patterns with these balanced clauses.

His first three statements are parallel in form, with the last clause of each returning to the verb of the first: 'hear me . . . that you may hear'; 'Believe me . . . that you may believe'; 'Censure me . . . that you may the better judge' ('censure' here means 'judge'). Then, after a rather looser declaration of his love for Caesar, he explains in a tight antithetical statement why he nevertheless killed him - 'not that I loved Caesar less, but that I loved Rome more' - and challenges his audience with his first rhetorical question (see p. 76):

Had you rather Caesar were living, and die all slaves, than that Caesar were dead, to live all free men? (23-5)

He develops his attitude to Caesar in a series of brief, parallel statements in which the last suddenly reverses the tenor of the previous ones - 'As Caesar loved me, I weep for him; . . . but, as he was ambitious, I slew him' - and then repeats the same series yet more tersely, concluding with three rhetorical questions, each of identical form and each followed by the same challenge: 'If any, speak; for him have I offended'.

It is often said that Brutus's speech is too intricate for the crowd, but this patterning can also make for clarity: everything falls into logical form, one is anticipating what is to come, and the individual clauses are short and simple. A more relevant criticism is that he speaks in abstract terms, using generalised concepts such as 'love', 'honour', 'valour' and 'ambition' without relating them to specific facts, so that they are soon forgotten when Antony substitutes words, and actions, which carry his meaning directly home to their hearts. But Brutus is in a difficult situation. He has admitted to himself that there is no evidence that Caesar would be tyrannical (II.i.10-34), and so has to speak in general terms and inspire his audience with his own enthusiasm for the great abstractions of freedom, honour and patriotism, without being specific about their meaning in the present situation or how they were being threatened. In the circumstances his speech is remarkably successful. He appeals to the crowd as 'Romans', evoking the great tradition of republican Rome to which they instinctively, if unreflectingly, respond; he associates himself with them as fellow countrymen and as 'lovers' of Caesar (13); he reminds them of his own reputation - 'Believe me for mine honour'; he flatters them by asking them to 'Censure me in your wisdom' - perhaps he really believes they can - and he gains their sympathy by declaring his own love for Caesar to be equal to theirs. His rhetorical questions all avoid the real, and awkward, question, for they assume that Caesar's ambition was a threat to freedom, but his uncritical listeners overlook this, and the question-begging form of his conclusion - 'Who is here so base . . . so rude . . . so vile . . . ?' - puts the answer into their mouths, 'None, Brutus, none'; who would claim to be base, rude or vile?

Brutus goes on to show his objectivity by telling the crowd that the reasons for Caesar's death are recorded in the archives, with a balanced estimate of his merits and offences (39–43), and promises a vaguely reassuring 'place in the commonwealth' to all. Finally he demonstrates that he is motivated entirely by principle by offering them his own life should his country need it (49–50).

The crowd responds enthusiastically, but these republican principles mean so little to them that they suggest rewarding Brutus for saving them from monarchy by making him king instead of Caesar:

> THIRD CITIZEN   Let him be Caesar.
> FOURTH CITIZEN   Caesar's better parts
> Shall be crowned in Brutus. (54–5)

CROWD

For them it is the person who matters, not the principle; they merely substitute one hero for another, as they had substituted Caesar for Pompey (I.i.39–57), and unwittingly Brutus has encouraged this: the only reason he gives them for accepting his assertion that Caesar was ambitious is his own honourable reputation –

> Believe me for mine honour, and have respect to mine honour, that you may believe. (14–16)

He is so unaware how impermanent its effect will be when he is no longer present that he begs the crowd to let him 'depart alone' and stay to hear Antony – ironically 'for my sake' (60)!

The 'gamesome' Antony is also a popular figure and is urged to 'go up into the public chair', but there is some ominous rumbling – ''Twere best he speak no harm of Brutus here!' – and wise nodding of heads:

> FIRST CITIZEN   This Caesar was a tyrant.
> THIRD CITIZEN   Nay, that's certain.
> We are blest that Rome is rid of him. (73–4)

Antony needs to be cautious. At first he presents himself merely as the mourning, but resigned, friend of Caesar, even denying any intention of praising him (78), and laying him to rest with a proverbial saying that would arouse further sympathy:

> The evil that men do lives after them,
> The good is oft interred with their bones;
> So let it be with Caesar. (79–81)

On the surface he adheres scrupulously to the conditions laid down by Brutus (III.i.245–51), repeating his charge that Caesar was ambitious, although 'If it were so' (83) implies the possibility of doubt, and the next line, 'And grievously hath Caesar answered it', points out that Caesar has certainly paid the full penalty. He acknowledges that he speaks 'under leave of Brutus and the rest', adding, 'For Brutus is an honourable man', although again there is a suspicion of irony in the too emphatic repetition of 'all' in the line that follows. Meekly, unobtrusively, he has already introduced the two statements that will form the keynote of his speech, and when he combines them –

> But Brutus says he was ambitious,
> And Brutus is an honourable man (90–91)

– he has in fact a terse summary of the substance of Brutus's speech: his assertion that Caesar was ambitious and his claim to be believed because of his honour. So far from attacking him directly Antony pretends to endorse what Brutus has said, repeating these lines like a refrain throughout the first section of his speech, while at the same time giving instances of Caesar's behaviour that suggest the contrary, culminating in Caesar's refusal of the crown offered him at the Lupercal. He is only doing what Brutus permitted – 'But speak all good you can devise of Caesar' (III.i. 246) – but the bland repetition of this refrain after each example is ironic in itself, and as the examples become more telling Antony points the irony. Caesar filled 'the general coffers' with the ransoms from his captives, 'Did this in Caesar seem ambitious?'; he wept when the poor cried, 'Ambition should be made of sterner stuff'; he thrice refused a 'kingly crown', 'Was this ambition?' Finally, with the addition of the contemptuous 'sure', the irony can be heard in the refrain itself – 'And sure he is an honourable man'. This nagging repetition is driving into the dullest mind his own scorn for this supposed honour, until with his final thrust,

> I fear I wrong the honourable men
> Whose daggers have stabbed Caesar, (155–6)

the Fourth Citizen voices their awareness: 'They were traitors. Honourable men!'

It is sometimes said that Brutus appeals to reason and Antony to emotion, but here it would be more accurate to say that Brutus appeals to abstract ideals and Antony to concrete facts, or supposed facts – we have only his word for it that Caesar wept when the poor were distressed, and Casca may well have been right that Caesar was reluctant to refuse the crown, but he did refuse it, and, as Antony reminds them (99), they all saw him do so. He describes his own technique, although not his intention, when he declares,

> I speak not to disprove what Brutus spoke,
> But here I am to speak what I do know. (104–5)

He presents selected facts, suited to the crowd's capacity and appealing to their self-interest, and directs them to the conclusion he wants them to draw.

But Antony also works directly on their emotions, breaking off in a display of grief that is no doubt genuinely felt but which he exploits – as he did with the conspirators – to stir the crowd's sympathy, bringing it home to them by his lament that they do not share his sorrow (106-7). The pause also enables him to observe their reactions, which develop rapidly from the reflective comment, 'Methinks there is much reason in his sayings' (after all the emphasis on Brutus's 'reasons' this is delightfully ironic) through a mixture of simple-minded reasoning,

> Marked ye his words? He would not take the crown;
> Therefore 'tis certain he was not ambitious, (116-17)

and sentimentality,

> Poor soul! His eyes are red as fire with weeping, (119)

to the first rumbling threat of revenge. 'If it be found so, some will dear abide it' (118). After less than a quarter of his speech Antony has won the argument.

He now turns to stirring up the crowd's fury against the conspirators, which he does characteristically by disclaiming any such intention:

> O masters, if I were disposed to stir
> Your hearts and minds to mutiny and rage,
> I should do Brutus wrong, and Cassius wrong,
> Who, you all know, are honourable men. (125-8)

While paying lip service to Brutus's conditions he puts the idea of mutiny into their minds and incites them all the more by pretending to restrain them. He adopts the same technique when he produces his master card, Caesar's will, refusing to read it while clearly indicating its nature. Hearing it the commoners

> would go and kiss dead Caesar's wounds,
> And dip their napkins in his sacred blood,
> Yea, beg a hair of him for memory. (136-8)

Calpurnia's prophetic dream has already been fulfilled in the sense she feared when the conspirators bathed their hands in Caesar's blood, and now Decius's deceitful interpretation of it (II.ii.83-90) is shown to have a degree of truth that Decius himself certainly did not intend: Brutus's symbolic gesture failed to turn the murder into a sacrifice, but the power of Antony's oratory is turning it into a martyrdom, so that Caesar's blood will be prized by the people as a precious relic. Continuing to express mock horror at the consequences should he read the will, while openly disclosing its contents –

> 'Tis good you know not that you are his heirs;
> For if you should, O, what would come of it! (149-50)

– he manipulates the crowd into insisting that it be read, forcing him to do precisely what he wants to do.

The contrast with Brutus's approach is again marked. Brutus had lectured them from a detached moral standpoint, Antony shares his emotions with them as equals; it is noticeable that while Antony uses the same initial form of address as Brutus (13, 77) he puts the more intimate term, 'Friends', first. Now in a telling reversal of Marullus's authoritarian rebuke – 'You blocks, you stones' (I.i.37) – he acknowledges them as fellow men: 'You are not wood, you are not stones, but men' (146). He pleads with them as 'gentle friends' (144) and adopts the form of address they use with each other, 'O masters' (125, compare 114). These words are reinforced by action when he descends from the pulpit, having first humbly asked their leave, and gathers them with him round the corpse of Caesar.

The intimate tone continues as he begins with a touching personal recollection:

> You all do know this mantle. I remember
> The first time ever Caesar put it on;
> 'Twas on a summer's evening in his tent. (177-9)

The mantle draws them together in fellowship with Caesar, while at the same time becoming a symbol of his military triumphs, for he first wore it on 'That day he overcame the Nervii'. Similarly, each carefully identified rent symbolises the treachery of the murderers. Antony, in fact, did not accompany Caesar on his campaign against the Nervii, and as he did not see the assassination he could not know where each conspirator stabbed; nevertheless, this is the most moving part of the speech for the audience as well as the crowd, for there is a considerable element of truth when he comes to the treachery of 'the well-beloved Brutus' (183) and recreates the poignancy of Caesar's final words:

> For when the noble Caesar saw him stab,
> Ingratitude, more strong than traitors' arms,
> Quite vanquished him. (191-3)

The vivid references to blood (185, 196, 199) continue the emphasis on the physical brutality of the murder and add a further strand to the web of symbolism that is woven round it. There is an obvious parallel between Pompey's statue, 'Which all the while ran blood' (196), and Caesar's statue running 'pure blood' in Calpurnia's dream, although its significance is ambiguous. It might signify that Pompey's death has been revenged – the bleeding of the statue suggests the folk belief that the corpse of a murdered man bled in the presence of the murderer – but Antony uses it to imply that the treacherous manner of Caesar's murder has led even his old enemy to sympathise with him. Antony draws his audience into even closer unity with himself and with the murdered Caesar,

> Then I, and you, and all of us fell down,
> Whilst bloody treason flourished over us, (198-9)

and with a final dramatic gesture flings off the mantle:

> Look you here!
> Here is himself, marred, as you see, with traitors. (203-4)

The effect on the crowd is overwhelming. Previously they had responded in varied ways as individuals, trying to 'consider rightly of the matter' (113); now there is only a concerted outburst of sorrow (205-9) followed by an explosion of fury:

> ALL   Revenge! About! Seek! Burn! Fire! Kill! Slay! Let not a traitor live! (211-12)

The crowd of reasonable, if simple-minded, individuals has become a passionate mob, roaring for revenge with one voice.

Antony's second object has been achieved. He has moved from giving concrete evidence that Caesar was not ambitious to exhibiting the physical reality of Caesar's corpse. As he says himself, 'I tell you that which you yourselves do know' – at least, what he persuades them to think they know –

> Show you sweet Caesar's wounds, poor poor dumb mouths,
> And bid them speak for me. (232-3)

We recall how he had prophesied 'blood and destruction' over Caesar's wounds,

> Which like dumb mouths do ope their ruby lips,
> To beg the voice and utterance of my tongue, (III.i.260-1)

and now he has

> put a tongue
> In every wound of Caesar that should move
> The stones of Rome to rise and mutiny (235-7)

- although he declares that it is Brutus, not he, who has the oratorical gifts to achieve this.

The contrast Antony draws here between himself and Brutus is profoundly ironic. It was his reputation for political naivete that misled Brutus into allowing him to speak, and now he exploits it with acute political subtlety, describing himself just as Brutus might have described him in order to emphasise his identity with the commoners as 'a plain blunt man, That love my friend' (225-6), and demonstrate his simple sincerity by contrasting his lack of 'wit', 'words' and 'worth' - 'the power of speech To stir men's blood' (228-30) - with the deceptive oratory of Brutus, who 'will, no doubt, with reasons answer you' (222). 'Reasons' has now become as degraded a term as 'honourable', and by inserting 'What private griefs they have, alas, I know not' (220) Antony implies that these reasons only mask the actual selfish motives.

To 'reasons' Antony opposes facts, or supposed facts, and he has one more fact to offer the crowd: 'You have forgot the will' (246). Nothing shows more clearly both the mindlessness of the mob and Antony's mastery over it than the way in which he makes them insist that he read the will; then makes them forget it and raises them to a pitch of grief and fury without its aid; and finally reminds them of it so that, by disclosing Caesar's bequests, he can leave them with a solid appeal to their self-interest that will survive when these heady emotions have begun to fade.

The reactions of a theatre audience to Antony's speech will be varied and complex. Whatever one feels about his deception of Brutus - and Brutus, after all, had deceived Caesar - one must admire the skill with which he effects it. The speech has an apparent spontaneity, he responds instinctively to the mood of the crowd, and yet it develops a firm overall structure as he moves from cautious ironic suggestion to forthright denunciation over the corpse of Caesar, and finally clinches his case by reading the will. Moreoever, do we not also share his delight in his own cunning, a delight that is evident, for example, in the humour of his mock alarm that he is wronging those 'honourable men' - 'I do fear it' (156) - in the sly interjection of 'alas' to suggest sorrow rather than anger when he implies they were motivated by 'private griefs' (220), and, above all, in his satisfaction at having turned the tables so neatly on Brutus? Antony knows that it is only Brutus's contempt for his abilities that has enabled him to address the crowd and he takes malicious pleasure in agreeing with this opinion, to his own advantage,

> I come not, friends, to steal away your hearts;
> I am no orator, as Brutus is, (223-4)

and speaks only the plain truth when he adds,

> and that they know full well
> That gave me public leave to speak of him. (226-7)

46

Yet his success results from those very attributes that Brutus despised (see p. 70).

But while one can appreciate Antony's satisfaction that Brutus's smugness should have rebounded so quickly upon him, one can hardly sympathise with the cool irresponsibility with which he contemplates the result of his oratory:

> Now let it work. Mischief, thou art afoot,
> Take thou what course thou wilt. (269-70)

It is he who has brought about the curse he prophesied; he has invoked the spirit of Caesar to arouse destructive forces against his enemies, but now not even he can control them, and he does not care. His elation continues after the servant tells him of Octavius's arrival,

> Fortune is merry,
> And in this mood will give us anything, (275-6)

but he is still the calculating opportunist, ready to exploit what fortune brings as he leaves to meet Octavius – unlike the conspirators, whose elation after the assassination betrayed them into wasting time with empty heroics. His mastery of the situation is expressed in the cool, ironic understatement with which he greets the news of Brutus's and Cassius's flight:

> Belike they had some notice of the people,
> How I had moved them. (279-80)

Act III, Scene iii

Summary
A mob murders Cinna the poet because he has the same name as one of the conspirators.

Commentary
Cinna's dream and his sense of foreboding add to the omens that accompany the assassination, but the main function of this scene is to show the irrational brutality of the force that Antony has unleashed. The degree to which the crowd has been transformed is underlined by the parallels with I.i. Roles are now reversed. Then it was Marullus who questioned the commoners in a domineering manner, now it is they who interrogate Cinna with brusque truculence. Like the Second Citizen in the earlier scene, Cinna replies humorously, implying that it is wiser to be a bachelor than a married man (16); either he mistakes their temper or tries to placate them with a joke. But this crowd is in no mood for joking. In I.i the Second Citizen had enjoyed raising a laugh against himself (see p 6). but his counterpart here, who must be a married man, chooses to take

Cinna's remark personally and threatens to strike him (17-19). Any excuse will do, he is only looking for trouble, as are the rest of them. At first they genuinely mistake Cinna for the conspirator, but when he protests that he is the poet, and a friend of Caesar, they do not care whether he is or not: 'It is no matter, his name's Cinna'. The commoners are now really 'worse than senseless things', as Marullus had called them, and liable to kill their allies as well as their opponents.

The murder of Cinna is a grotesque example of the importance of names in the play (see p.72), and the cynical comment, 'Pluck but his name out of his heart, and turn him going' (34-5) might be seen as a grim burlesque of Brutus's wish to come by Caesar's spirit - 'Caesarism' - without dismembering Caesar (II.i.169-70).

Act IV, Scene i

Summary
Antony, Octavius and Lepidus, the Triumvirate that now controls Rome, decide which of their enemies must be killed. Having sent Lepidus to fetch Caesar's will so that they can reduce his bequests to the Roman people, Antony proposes that they should dispose of him when he has served their purpose. Octavius grudgingly agrees, and they prepare to meet the forces that Brutus and Cassius are raising against them.

Commentary
This scene, like the previous one, shows the malign consequences of Antony's triumph. The mood is very different, but the Triumvirs are also engaged in murder. Antony sets the tone with his matter-of-fact opening statement, 'These many then shall die', and the cold-blooded trading of the life of his nephew for that of Lepidus's brother is at least as distasteful as the murderous fury of the mob. Families have been divided, and the reason for these ruthless political murders is shown by Octavius's final speech; they are 'bayed about with many enemies' and do not know whom to trust:

> And some that smile have in their hearts, I fear,
> Millions of mischiefs. (49-51)

Antony appears at his worst in this scene. The insincerity of his wooing of the crowd is made abundantly clear by his intention to cheat them of the legacies in Caesar's will (8-9), and his attitude to his closest colleagues is equally cynical. Lepidus is merely a 'property' (40), something to be used, and once he has taken the blame for their unpopular actions (20) they can

> turn him off,
> Like to the empty ass, to shake his ears,
> And graze in commons. (25-7)

Antony combines a self-seeking that surpasses that of the worst of the conspirators with something of the overbearing manner of Brutus when he lectures Octavius at unnecessary length about Lepidus. We have already seen that he feels he must control affairs for the youthful Octavius (III.i.289-90), and he reminds him here of his inexperience (18). But Octavius on his first appearance shows considerable independence of mind. He is more objective in his assessment of Lepidus, and while he acquiesces in Antony's proposal he does not show much respect for his opinion: 'You may do you will' (27). He is as casually ruthless as the others in proscribing their enemies – 'Prick him down, Antony' (3) – and his final speech shows a shrewd awareness of political realities.

These realities are revealed here in their most basic and brutal form. The contrast between Antony's readiness to sacrifice his nephew and Brutus's insistence that Antony's own life should be spared emphasises both the former's callousness and the latter's lack of realism. Antony's attitude to the commoners and to Lepidus may bear out Brutus's fear of the effect of power on ambitious men – that they humble themselves in order to climb to power and having achieved it spurn those who helped them to rise (II.i.21-7) – but by averting the danger that Caesar might be thus corrupted Brutus has only succeeded in opening the way for a much worse tyranny.

Act IV, Scene ii

Summary
Brutus and Cassius meet near Sardis with the forces each has been raising, but they have now fallen out and withdraw into Brutus's tent to continue their dispute in private.

Commentary
The new scene of military activity is conveyed economically by the drum that announces the return of Lucilius, Brutus's lieutenant, from a meeting with Cassius, and by the curt martial orders (1-2, 32-6).

The latent disunity among the Triumvirs apparent in the previous scene is paralleled by the open differences between Brutus and Cassius. Brutus is so incensed by some action of Cassius or his officers that he offends against propriety by criticising Cassius to his own servant, Pindarus, and when Lucilius describes the formal coolness of his reception by Cassius he characteristically seizes this opportunity to moralise. His contrast between 'plain and simple faith' and the insincere 'tricks' of 'enforced ceremony' (20-2) recalls his objection to the conspirators' taking a formal oath, but while this reflects his own honest openness he seems hasty in his condemnation. Cassius's outburst, 'Most noble brother, you have done me wrong' (37), with no preliminary courtesies, is equally characteristic, and inevitably provokes Brutus to appeal to his unblemished reputation: 'Judge me, you gods; wrong I mine enemies?' – it might have occurred to him that it was just such highmindedness that had prompted his disastrous generosity to Antony. It is Brutus, however, who keeps sufficient control of himself to suggest that they withdraw so that their armies are not disconcerted by seeing the two generals at odds.

Act IV, Scene iii

Some editions have no change of scene at this point, the line numbering continuing from that of IV.ii.

Summary

The dispute continues in Brutus's tent, with Cassius complaining that Brutus has been too severe in executing justice on their own supporters, and Brutus accusing Cassius of taking bribes himself. The quarrel becomes increasingly trivial until Brutus claims that Cassius refused to send him money, and Cassius, distressed by the violence of their dispute, offers him his life instead. Their reconciliation is completed when a poet breaks in to urge them to be friends, and Brutus tells Cassius that his ill mood has been caused by the news of Portia's death.

With their lieutenants they review the situation: the Triumvirs have put many senators to death, including Cicero, and are leading a strong force against them. Brutus proposes that they advance to Philippi; Cassius objects, but again gives way.

They part affectionately, and Brutus settles to read when the ghost of Caesar enters, telling him that they will meet at Philippi. Brutus sends his attendants to tell Cassius to advance with his forces early in the morning.

Commentary

The scene is a classic study of the nature of a quarrel, beginning with particular grievances but developing into a wider clash of personalities that brings into the open the differences between Brutus and Cassius which both have been tacitly evading. Cassius again takes the lead, complaining that Brutus has ignored his plea on behalf of Lucius Pella, and has been unreasonable in condemning what he considers a trivial offence when they cannot afford to alienate their friends (7-8). Brutus replies by attacking Cassius's lack of principle, charging him with selling profitable offices in exchange for bribes (9-12). Already the dispute has become a clash between political expediency and moral idealism, perhaps moral rigidity. Now that Cassius openly states that they cannot afford to be too scrupulous, Brutus rounds on him. His moral probity may be admirable, but one must also recognise his lack of realism, not only in antagonising one of their supporters, but in supposing that their cause is so unblemished that they would otherwise sully its purity; he persists in refusing to recognise the very mixed motives of the other conspirators:

> What villain touched his body, that did stab,
> And not for justice? (20-1)

Again, one may suspect that this extravagant insistence on the justice of their cause is an unconscious attempt to still his own misgivings about its justification, especially when he adds charges against Caesar that have not previously been mentioned; he said nothing of 'justice' (21) or 'supporting robbers' (23) when he originally considered why Caesar must be killed (II.i.10-34). His inner conflict is still evident in the admiration with which he describes Caesar as 'the foremost man of all this world' (22) and refers to him by his personal name, 'great Julius' (19) - significantly only the second time it is used in the play, the first being by Antony (III.i.204).

Cassius, too, has reached breaking point. Indignant at this moral presumption, especially at Brutus's reference to 'chastisement' (17), for the first time he openly challenges his practical ability, and not without good cause:

> I am a soldier, I,
> Older in practice, abler than yourself
> To make conditions. (30-2)

The quarrel now sinks to the level of childish contradictions -

> BRUTUS   Go to! You are not, Cassius.
> CASSIUS   I am.
> BRUTUS   I say you are not; (33-5)

threats - 'Have mind upon your health; tempt me no farther'; wild abuse - 'Shall I be frighted when a madman stares?'; and cheap mockery -

> from this day forth
> I'll use you for my mirth, yea, for my laughter,
> When you are waspish. (48-50)

Righteous anger has degenerated into spiteful gibes. It is characteristic of such quarrels that Brutus accuses Cassius of the very fault to which he is himself most prone -

> Must I observe you? Must I stand and crouch
> Under your testy humour? (45-6)

- and equally characteristic that the original issue is forgotten and they are squabbling about whether Cassius said an 'elder' or a 'better' soldier (51-8) - in fact he said both.

Cassius is clearly shaken by Brutus's unexpected venom, and it is to his credit that he makes the first move towards a reconciliation by withdrawing this claim - 'Did I say better?' - while Brutus remains sulkily unresponsive - 'If you did, I care not' - and launches a sustained reproof of Cassius for refusing to send him money. He speaks from a lofty sense of moral superiority – 'armed so strong in honesty' (67) – that is shot through with contradictions. He has condemned Cassius for the methods he uses to raise money, but nevertheless expects a share of it because he cannot bring himself to use similar methods – 'For I can raise no money by vile means' (71)! Only a man whose judgement is clouded by his own self-esteem could be so unreasonable, and while he speaks this in the heat of argument it is symptomatic of his situation as a whole. For the success of their cause he has to temporise with his moral principles, and the contradictions result from his refusal to admit this. Thus he continues to speak loftily of money as 'vile trash', and prides himself on his inability to wring it from 'the hard hands of peasants', while complaining that he has not been sent his share.

But Brutus is also beginning to soften, in a condescending way. He implies that this was untypical of Cassius, using their personal names in what is now a reproach rather than an accusation (77-82), and Cassius moves the dispute to its final stage by giving up any attempt to defend himself – 'A friend should bear his friend's infirmities' (86) – and complaining instead that Brutus is being unkind – 'You love me not' (89). The original issues no longer matter, only the breach that has developed between them; in more domestic circumstances the quarrel would end in a flood of tears. Brutus is stiffly reserved, never responding easily to direct emotion – 'I do not like your faults' (89) – and then Cassius does produce the tears, perhaps literally so: 'O, I could weep My spirit from mine eyes' (99-100). He is

> Hated by one he loves; braved by his brother;
> Checked like a bondman; all his faults observed,
> Set in a note-book, learned, and conned by rote,
> To cast into my teeth. (96-9)

Bitterly Cassius sums up Brutus's precise moralism and to it opposes naked emotion, baring his breast and offering his dagger:

> Strike as thou didst at Caesar; for I know
> When thou didst hate him worst, thou lovedst him better
> Than ever thou lovedst Cassius. (105-7)

One realises how much Brutus's reference to 'great Julius' (19) must have stung him. For a moment the whole action of the play becomes personalised. Cassius has already indicated that his envy of Caesar includes a jealousy of the love between Caesar and Brutus (I.ii.315-17, and see p. 71) and it is to an open declaration of that jealousy that their quarrel leads.

Brutus at last relents. At first he can only unbend so far as to be indulgent to Cassius's failings – 'Do what you will, dishonour shall be humour' (109) – but finally admits, 'When I spoke that, I was ill-tempered too'

(116); and Cassius is amazed at such a confession from the immaculate Brutus: 'Do you confess so much?' His final outburst has the theatrical quality we expect of Cassius, but there is no doubt about the genuineness of the emotion here. Even after they are reconciled he can only ejaculate, 'O Brutus!', and wants further reassurance of his love as he confesses to an inherited ill-temper, and Brutus – 'your Brutus' – responds tenderly (118-23). This emotional conclusion is relieved by the bizarre intrusion of the poet; Cassius is amused, welcoming the release of tension, but Brutus's sense of propriety is offended (133-8), although the poet's doggerel is a not unfitting comment on the childishness of some his own recent behaviour.

This quarrel is often absurd and petty, but its openness and honest feeling compares favourably with the concealed rivalry between the Triumvirs. It forces us to reconsider our earlier impression of Cassius and his attitude to Brutus. Brutus comes less well out of it, but it may be a relief to find that he can behave in so human a manner, and he explains to Cassius why he has lost his usual self-control: Portia is dead (147). He regards her death with the fortitude of a Stoic. Stoicism is the 'philosophy' to which Cassius refers (145), the central principle of which is the exercise of severe self-discipline. For a Stoic the only thing of value to a man is his own virtue, so he accepts what fate brings as inevitable and is unmoved by 'accidental evils' (145-6); a little later Brutus explains to Messala how he disciplines himself to accept the inevitable:

> With meditating that she must die once,
> I have the patience to endure it now. (191-2)

So Brutus states the fact of her death curtly, but one feels both the strength of his grief and the self-control with which he restrains it in the brevity of his statement. It is Cassius who is the more demonstrative (150-2), and he cannot escape the thought even after their lieutenants have entered – 'Portia, art thou gone?' (166) – while Brutus turns at once to practical affairs.

A textual problem arises when Brutus tells Messala that he has had no news of his wife (181-4), so that Messala has to tell him of Portia's death. If Shakespeare intended both reports of her death to be included, Brutus can only be pretending ignorance in order to impress his subordinates with the fortitude with which he receives the news, but even if Brutus were thought capable of such deliberate deceit it is unlikely that he would have practised it before Cassius, who knows the truth. It is generally assumed, therefore, that Messala originally announced Portia's death and that Shakespeare omitted to cancel this passage when he used it instead as the explanation of Brutus's bad temper. If the later passage is omitted, then 'Well, to our work alive' (196) follows naturally from the report of Cicero's death (178-80).

When they discuss tactics the familiar pattern is repeated. Brutus gives what seem sensible reasons for their advancing on Philippi (203-17), as well as the general reflection that

> There is a tide in the affairs of men,
> Which, taken at the flood, leads on to fortune;
> Omitted, all the voyage of their life
> Is bound in shallows and in miseries; (218-21)

but the satisfaction of Antony and Octavius at this decision (V. i.1-12) suggests that he would have been better advised to heed Cassius's objections instead of once more brushing them aside. They part emotionally, Cassius still feeling the effects of the quarrel:

> Never come such division 'tween our souls!
> Let it not, Brutus. (235-6)

The balance of our sympathies tilts towards Brutus again when we see him once more in his private life. There is a natural, easy courtesy when he insists that Varro and Claudius sleep, and in the touch of humour against himself with which he confesses his forgetfulness to Lucius: 'Look, Lucius, here's the book I sought for so' (252). He is sympathetic when he asks him to play (256-66), and when Lucius falls asleep, as in II.i, instead of waking him he gently removes his instrument in case he should break it (271-2). It is typical that he should carry a book in the pocket of his gown while campaigning, with the leaf turned down (273) so that he can resume reading as soon as he has a respite from public affairs. Such details admit us intimately into his civilised, scholarly personality. The song adds to the sense of harmony with a quiet melancholy. There is a general somnolence as Claudius and Varro sleep, Lucius speaks 'drowsily' (240) and even the tune is 'sleepy' (267). Brutus settles to read, the taper burns dimly (275), and the ghost enters.

The details that have built up this peaceful atmosphere – the silence, the drowsiness, the dim light (lamps were supposed to burn dim at the approach of a ghost) – have also prepared for its entry, as unwelcome thoughts slip into our minds in moments of relaxation and destroy our tranquility. It is an enigmatic encounter. Only the stage direction indicates that this is the ghost of Caesar, and the audience would not know this until Brutus identifies it shortly before his death (V. v. 17). The ghost says only that it is his 'evil spirit' (282). It is not a ghostly reproduction of the living Caesar but a 'monstrous apparition' that might be a god, an angel, or a devil (277-9). It might even be a hallucination produced by Brutus's weary mind from his repressed feelings of guilt about the murder; this could be suggested by its disappearance when Brutus has 'taken heart' (288), although actual ghosts were also thought to vanish when they were challenged. Its message is also enigmatic, if vaguely ominous: Brutus will see it at Philippi. But whether it is an actual ghost or an emanation from Brutus's troubled mind is of little consequence; symbolically, it is clearly the spirit of Caesar that Brutus has failed to destroy, although whether it survives as a 'god' or a 'devil' is left uncertain.

Brutus's brief intermission of peace is destroyed, as he has destroyed his own domestic peace and betrayed the trust of Caesar by accepting the terrible duty of murdering him. He is at first alarmed but soon collects himself, and his matter-of-fact reply (285, 287) expresses his readiness to accept what is to come. He questions his attendants to confirm that they have heard and seen nothing and addresses himself resolutely to the coming action.

Act V, Scene i

Summary
Antony and Octavius prepare for battle, Octavius insisting that his forces take the right-hand side. The rival leaders parley, exchanging insults and challenges. When Antony and Octavius have left, Cassius expresses his misgivings about the coming action and he and Brutus agree to commit suicide if they are defeated.

Commentary
There are more signs of incipient rivalry between Antony and Octavius, and the latter is beginning to assert himself. He points out that his assessment of the enemy's intentions was correct (1-4) and claims the place of honour in the order of battle (18). His terse statement admits no argument: 'I do not cross you; but I will do so' (20) means that he does not intend to contradict Antony, but nevertheless will take the right, but it also anticipates future events when the two come to open conflict and Antony is defeated.

The parley before battle, a common practice in mediaeval warfare, supplements the limited resources that Shakespeare had for presenting a physical battle with a verbal confrontation between the opposing leaders. Antony and Octavius seem to have the better of it. In the interchange of contrasting words and blows (27-38) Octavius's mocking reference to Brutus's love of words and Antony's to his treachery must strike home, recalling to Brutus his hatred of the deception he had to practise. His and Cassius's taunts are ineffectual compared with the pointed bitterness of Antony's account of the deceit and violence of the assassination:

> when your vile daggers
> Hacked one another in the sides of Caesar. (39-40)

The conspirators are no longer the hunters (III.i.205) but the hounds (41), and this comparison combines with the description of Casca as 'a cur' (43) and Cassius's reference to Antony's honeyed words (33-5) to recall the similar combination of imagery with which Caesar had condemned flattery immediately before his murder (III.i.39-46). Cassius is stung for the first, and only, time to reproach Brutus for his misjudgement:

> Now Brutus thank yourself;
> This tongue had not offended so today,
> If Cassius might have ruled. (45-7)

Both the conspirators' treachery and their errors are being brought home to them, and while Cassius tries to retort by taunting Octavius with his youth – 'a peevish schoolboy' – and Antony with his former reputation as 'a masker and a reveller' (61-2), he has always known this to be untrue, and Antony can turn the insult casually aside with cheerful contempt, 'Old Cassius still!'

Antony and Octavius also seem the more intent on action. Octavius has little patience with this bickering, 'Come, come, the cause' (48), and his resolute challenges (50-5, 64-6) contrast with the rather desperate recklessness of Cassius after they have parted:

> Why now, blow wind, swell billow, and swim bark!
> The storm is up, and all is on the hazard. (67-8)

The mood in Brutus's and Cassius's camp is subdued. Cassius registers with Messala his opposition to Brutus's decision

> to set
> Upon one battle all our liberties (75-6)

by advancing on Philippi, and his misgivings are increased by the ominous portent that their army has been deserted by the eagles that had accompanied it – eagles symbolised victory, the standards of Roman legions were bronze eagles. They have been replaced by carrion birds that feed on corpses, and this 'canopy most fatal' (88) joins with the earlier appearance of Caesar's ghost to Brutus to give a sense of impending disaster. It is the more striking in that as an Epicurean Cassius would not have believed in portents (77-8, see p.16), but is now being persuaded to change his opinion.

The possibility of failure is also making Brutus modify his philosophical views. In theory, the Stoic can have no reason for committing suicide 'For fear of what might fall' (105), since external disasters cannot affect the one thing that matters to him, his own virtue (see p.52). Moreover, suicide is impious since the Stoic believed that man's fate was determined by the gods; he should not anticipate the time appointed for the end of his life – 'prevent The time of life' (105-6) – but patiently await

> the providence of some high powers
> That govern us below. (107-8)

Even so, the Romans considered it more honourable for a defeated general to kill himself than to submit to the shame of captivity, showing a stoical fortitude, in a more general sense, by the courage with which he took his own life, as had Brutus's father-in-law, the Stoic Cato (102, see p. 5). Thus Brutus's decision not to go bound to Rome can be seen as a noble resolution – he 'bears too great a mind' (113).

A sense of fate hangs over their discussion:

> this same day
> Must end the work the ides of March begun. (113-14)

Even the fact that it is Cassius's birthday (72; see V.iii.23-5) gives it a certain appropriateness as the day that will decide his fate. He claims to be 'fresh of spirit' (91), but their preparations are for defeat, not victory. They take a solemn farewell of each other, the repetition giving it a ritual quality (117-22), and the wry reflection, 'If we do meet again, why, we shall smile' (118, 121) increases the pathos rather than conveying any feeling of hope. There is no optimism in Brutus's final words,

> it sufficeth that the day will end,
> And then the end is known, (125-6)

only Stoic resignation, and probably relief that the sorry business will at last be finished with.

Act V, Scene ii

Summary
Observing the low morale in Octavius's forces, Brutus intends to overthrow them with a sudden attack, and sends Messala to tell Cassius to advance.

Commentary
The alarum, a trumpet call to arms, is probably accompanied by sounds of battle, and by fighting on stage to separate Brutus's last exit from his immediate re-entry. Shakespeare presents the battle through a series of short scenes in different parts of the field, showing the alternations of fortune; here there is a brief hope that Brutus and Cassius will gain the victory.

Act V, Scene iii

Summary
Cassius's forces have been put to flight by Antony. Cassius sends Titinius to discover the identity of a distant body of troops and, thinking that he has been captured, commits suicide. Messala enters with Titinius, telling

him that the battle is evenly balanced as Brutus has defeated Octavius. Seeing the dead Cassius, Messala goes to inform Brutus, while Titinius kills himself. Brutus enters and pays a hasty tribute to Cassius before leaving to renew the battle.

Commentary
The scene conveys the confusion and uncertainty of battle, and the optimism of the previous scene is soon extinguished. Titinius may be right in claiming that Brutus attacked prematurely (5-7), but on this occasion his tactics were successful – even though his troops wasted their advantage in pillaging – and now it is Cassius's too hasty reaction that leads to his suicide; one recalls how he had jumped to conclusions when he thought Popilius was betraying the conspiracy to Caesar (III.i.13-22). His error in too readily believing the worst is due to no small extent to the pessimism evident in V. i. While Pindarus watches Titinius he reflects,

> This day I breathed first: time is come round,
> And where I did begin, there shall I end;
> My life is run his compass; (23-5)

as Messala says, the error is the offspring of his melancholy (66-71). He dies on the sword that killed Caesar –

> Caesar, thou art revenged,
> Even with the sword that killed thee (45-6)

– and Brutus makes clear the symbolic significance of this:

> O Julius Caesar, thou art mighty yet!
> Thy spirit walks abroad, and turns our swords
> In our own proper entrails. (94-6)

Titinius comments, 'Alas, thou hast misconstrued every thing' (84), and as all Cassius's schemes finally collapse in error and confusion one might see here a more general reference to his misreading of the political situation in Rome; but as his fortunes decline the more sympathetic view of his character that has been developing since the quarrel reaches its climax in the tributes at his death. To Brutus he is 'The last of all the Romans' (99), and Titinius gives him a splendid epitaph,

> O setting sun,
> As in thy red rays thou dost sink tonight,
> So in his red blood Cassius' day is set.
> The sun of Rome is set, (60-3)

sealing it with the supreme tribute of killing himself with Cassius's sword.

Act V, Scene iv

Summary
Brutus's forces are making a last stand. Cato's son is killed and Lucilius diverts the soldiers seeking to capture Brutus by pretending to be Brutus himself.

Commentary
There is probably more fighting on stage at the beginning of the scene as otherwise Brutus would again have to enter immediately after his last exit. The hope he expressed then has clearly been dashed. His followers can only demonstrate their courage and their loyalty to the republic as Cato proudly proclaims the name of his father and Lucilius shows his devotion to Brutus by preventing his capture. He forecasts Brutus's suicide and emphasises its nobility (21-3). Antony's reception of Lucilius shows unexpected magnanimity, mixed with his characteristic shrewdness: 'I had rather have Such men my friends than enemies' (28-9).

Act V, Scene v

Summary
Brutus asks each of his followers in turn to kill him, but they refuse. He takes a last farewell of them as the sounds of battle come nearer until at a final alarm close at hand they fly. Brutus detains Strato, who has been asleep and does not know that the others have refused to kill him, and persuades him to hold his sword while he runs on it. Octavius and Antony enter; the former promises to take all who have served Brutus into his service and the latter pays a generous tribute to his virtues.

Commentary
The last gleam of hope is extinguished with the torch of Statilius - Statilius had volunteered to go through the enemy lines to Brutus's camp, but although he signalled that all was well there, he failed to return. The spirit of Caesar has hung over Brutus throughout the battle, and it is the second appearance of the ghost that has persuaded him that his time is come (17-20). Suicide now appears as acceptance of divine fate rather than rebellion against it (see pp. 55-6):

> It is more worthy to leap in ourselves,
> Than tarry till they push us. (24-5)

The sense of destiny is strong as Brutus resigns himself to death:

> Night hangs upon mine eyes; my bones would rest,
> That have but laboured to attain this hour. (41-2)

Behind this lies the Stoic principle that since death is inevitable it is towards death that all men labour (see IV.iii.191-2); but there is also a great weariness that is spiritual rather than physical, and a sense of failure. It is only with his own death that the spirit of Caesar can be laid to rest:

> Caesar, now be still;
> I killed not thee with half so good a will. (50-1)

All that is left to him is the personal honour of not surrendering to his enemies - as Strato says,

> For Brutus only overcame himself,
> And no man else hath honour by his death (56-7)

- and the devotion of his followers, which is strongly emphasised by their horror at the thought of killing him even at his own request:

> My heart doth joy that yet in all my life
> I found no man but he was true to me. (34-5)

At least on these personal grounds Brutus can claim,

> I shall have glory by this losing day,
> More than Octavius and Mark Antony
> By this vile conquest shall attain unto. (36-8)

Antony's praise of Brutus (68-75) is in striking contrast to their previous meeting; Shakespeare is using him to utter an objective tribute to Brutus with which to end the play, but this does not necessarily make him inconsistent, since he can afford to be generous now that Brutus is dead. He distinguishes his motives from those of the other conspirators (69-72) and emphasises his nobility - 'gentle' (73) means 'noble'. He expresses this in terms of the Elizabethan belief that the human constitution, along with all the physical world, was composed of the four basic elements - fire, air, earth and water - which when mixed in equal proportions produced the perfect man. In creating Brutus, Nature might claim to have approached this ideal of the balanced personality (73-5), equable and self-controlled, with no one element dominating. We have seen Brutus as a man of culture, a scholar, gentle in his domestic life but stern and resolute in action and calm in a crisis. That is not to say he has no faults, and perhaps serious ones, but the moment of his death is not the time to dwell on these.

3 THEMES AND ISSUES

3.1 THE POLITICAL THEME

Julius Caesar is a political play, but it does not make any explicit judgement about the political issues involved. It uses the conflict between republicanism and monarchy in Rome to explore human character in relation to political action, but on the specifically constitutional question it remains neutral. Shakespeare's handling of the storm and its accompanying portents is particularly significant on this point. In *Macbeth,* for instance, there is no question that similar cosmic upheavals express divine displeasure at the overthrow of legitimate monarchy, but in Rome there is as yet no legitimate monarch. Shakespeare gives equal weight to the interpretations of Cassius and Calpurnia (see pp.15, 25), and even among the conspirators, while Cassius sees the 'monstrous' prodigies as a reflection of the 'monstrous' domination of Rome by one man (I.iii.62–71), for Brutus it is conspiracy that is 'monstrous' (II.i.81).

Both sides of the political conflict are given eloquent advocates, but they are deliberately balanced so that our sympathies are constantly swayed from one side to the other. Moveover, the nature of the advocacy often tells against the advocate himself: Cassius's attack on Caesar reveals his malicious envy; Caesar's insistence on his authority reveals his arrogance; in justifying the assassination to himself Brutus suggests the weakness of the conspirators' case by the tortuous nature of his reasoning; Antony reawakens a sense of the greatness of Caesar but at the same time shows his own unprincipled cunning and thirst for revenge. Shakespeare is less interested in the cases these speakers present than in the ways in which they expose their own characters as they present them.

The play is exceptional among Shakespeare's tragedies in having four leading characters of roughly equal stature, all of whom can arouse both considerable sympathy and strong aversion; and all of them are least attractive in their political roles. One sees the subtle methods of persuasion in both private lobbying and public meetings; the sounding out of potential supporters and neutralising of opponents; the techniques of the demagogue when Caesar refuses the offered crown and Antony woos the crowd in the forum; the promotion of a 'cult of personality' – of blind faith in the person of the leader – as Caesar and his flatterers foster his public image; the use of deceit by Cassius with his fabricated letters, more subtly by Decius in persuading Caesar to go to the Senate, and most subtly of all by Antony when he exploits his agreement with Brutus to turn the crowd against him; the cynical exercise of power by the Triumvirs in their pro-scriptions, by Antony in scheming against Lepidus – to which Octavius assents – and in the methods used by Cassius to raise money – which Brutus must ultimately accept, even if he refuses to use them himself. As the play proceeds political action is reduced to a continual manoeuvring for power: the autocracy of Caesar is overthrown only to be replaced by the worse tyranny of the Triumvirs, and even as they are establishing their grip on Rome the latent disunity is revealed that will eventually lead to further power struggles. Politics, it seems, is a dirty business, yet it is a business in which men must participate if they are not merely to acquiesce in wrong, on whichever side wrong is thought to lie.

Not only do our sympathies fluctuate, but often it is difficult to decide whether one is sympathising or not: how does one balance esteem for Brutus's high principles against dislike of his self-righteousness, or sympathy with Antony's grief against disapproval – but also admiration and enjoy-ment – of the cunning with which he exploits it. It is such ambiguities that have led *Julius Caesar* to be called a 'problem play'. One may decide, as some critics have done, that one side is more clearly in the right, or one may conclude that as a whole the play reveals the moral complexity of political action, in which even the most well-meaning man is likely to go astray; indeed, that it is his very virtues that lead him astray: it is this that makes *Julius Caesar* a tragedy.

3.2 THE TRAGIC HERO

There is even disagreement about who is the hero of the play. Its full title is *The Tragedy of Julius Caesar*, and in all Shakespeare's other tragedies the character named in the title is the protagonist. Caesar certainly has the potential for a tragic hero. He fulfils the mediaeval concept of tragedy as the story of the fall of a great man from prosperity to adversity, and he is akin to many of the heroes of Greek tragedy in that his fall is brought about by pride, or 'hubris', the sin of claiming to have risen above hu-manity to equality with the gods; it is punished by the gods as Caesar might seem to be punished when he is killed at the moment when his pride reaches its zenith and he is equating himself with Olympus (III.i.74). It would be quite exceptional, however, for the hero to be killed half-way through the play, and if this were the tragic climax there would be a considerable slackening of interest, with the second half concerned only with the revenge of his murder. It is true that Caesar's spirit continues to dominate the play after his death, and this links it with the Elizabethan and Jacobean 'revenge' tragedies such as Tourneur's *Revenger's Tragedy* and Shakespeare's own *Hamlet*, but in revenge tragedy the original victim is not the hero. He is killed before the action begins and his ghost incites the hero to take revenge, the action culminating in the death both of the revenger and of those guilty of the murder.

The chief difficulty in regarding Caesar as the hero, however, is that we have been unable to sympathise with him sufficiently for his death to excite genuinely tragic emotions, moving though it is. We have had only occasional glimpses of his humanity, and even his greatness is not fully convincing until after his death. With Brutus, however, we are able to sympathise from his first appearance. We may disapprove of his decision that Caesar must be killed, but we know his own tormenting misgivings about it. He is the only character who suffers an internal conflict and into whose mind we are admitted so that we can share it. We may disapprove, but we can 'feel with', which is what 'sympathy' means; and his death is the natural tragic climax of the play.

3.3 IDEALISM AND POLITICS

It is also on Brutus that the central themes of the play are focused: the morality of political action and the conflict between public responsibility and private loyalties. He is a classic example of the liberal idealist who becomes involved in politics. As soon as he joins the conspiracy he is forced to compromise his ideals, accepting the necessity for deception and for enlisting the support of men whose motives are less pure than his own (see pp. 19-22). We are torn between sympathy with his regret that such methods must be used and exasperation that he should often either not recognise or deliberately shut his eyes to their nature as he continues to insist on the unsullied nobility of their cause and his own moral superiority, a self-contradiction that comes to a head in his quarrel with Cassius (see pp. 49-51). While Antony deceives others, Brutus deceives himself. For him, as much as for Antony, the end must justify the means.

To the fundamental question of whether the preservation of Roman liberties (the end) justifies the murder of Caesar (the means) the play gives no conclusive answer, and it is complicated by the peculiar nature of Brutus's reasoning. He concludes that Caesar must be killed not because he shows signs of becoming a tyrant but from fear of how he might change once he is crowned. The critic, Ernest Schanzer has argued that Brutus's concern about how Caesar might be corrupted shows that he is not opposed to monarchy merely on principle, but if Brutus believes that Caesar is exercising his virtually regal powers with moderation he must attach enormous significance to the title of king to suppose that the granting of it to Caesar would produce so radical a change in his nature. Brutus is an idealist not only in his lofty moral principles but in being moved by ideas: the very idea of kingship is abhorrent to him, and the general principle that men are corrupted by power weighs more with him than any specific evidence as to whether or not Caesar would be corrupted (II.i.21-7). His argument is sometimes justified by Lord Acton's maxim, 'Power tends to corrupt, and absolute power corrupts absolutely', although Brutus seems not to have noticed that power has even tended to corrupt Caesar.

It is clearly unjust to kill a man for what he might do in the future, but Brutus is in a dilemma. If he is persuaded that Roman liberty is threatened, it would be wrong not to act; the liberal idealist cannot escape responsibility by washing his hands of the dirty work of politics, and it is to Brutus's credit that having come to a decision he goes through with it in spite of the distress it causes him. As Schanzer has pointed out, Brutus is not the traditional ineffectual idealist: once his mind is made up he is firm and decisive, and steadier than Cassius in a crisis (III.i.13-24); he gives sensible reasons for his three major errors – the sparing of Antony and permitting him to address the crowd, and the advance on Philippi; he is initially successful in battle; and to save Rome from monarchy he is prepared to kill his best friend.

Moreover, the audience's judgement must be affected by the autocratic way in which Caesar is behaving, his contemptuous attitude to the Senate (II.ii.66-7; III.i.32), and his refusal to listen to pleas on behalf of Publius Cimber, as well as by the ominous fate of Marullus and Flavius. We might conclude that on his own arguments Brutus is not justified, but that on the evidence of the play there is a very real threat to Roman liberties. It has been suggested, in fact, that his error is in failing to realise that it is already too late to save the republic: Caesar's power is too entrenched, and the people are ready to accept a monarchy – they even propose that Brutus be crowned (III.ii.54-5) – so that, as Plutarch thought, Rome is no longer governable except by a strong man exercising absolute authority. This reading of the play is given support by the symbolic dominance of the spirit of Caesar after his murder, as if 'Caesarism' – absolute rule by one man – could not be destroyed merely by killing Caesar. This spirit certainly affects the action in the second half of the play by contributing to the pessimistic fatalism of the conspirators, which prompts Cassius's error in assuming the worst when he is told that Titinius is captured (see p. 57), and perhaps influences Brutus's decision 'to set Upon one battle all [their] liberties' so that the outcome will be settled quickly, one way or the other (V.i.75-6, 125-6). But that does not mean that their cause was doomed from the start, or that Cassius was wrong when he declared,

> The fault, dear Brutus, is not in our stars,
> But in ourselves, that we are underlings, (I.ii.140-1)

even though the course of events persuades Cassius to change his opinion

(V.i.77–9). Caesar's spirit is not an independent force but depends for its power on the feelings and actions of living men. It weighs most heavily on Brutus because of his love for Caesar, and it is ineffective until it is revived by Antony. Until Antony inflames the crowd with the memory of Caesar, Brutus is able to persuade them that 'This Caesar was a tyrant' (III.ii.73). It is Brutus who defines most accurately the relation of character to fate in *Julius Caesar*,

> There is a tide in the affairs of men,
> Which, taken at the flood, leads on to fortune; (IV.iii.218–9)

but, ironically, it is Antony who seizes the opportunity, and Brutus who gives it to him by his errors of judgement.

Brutus's cardinal mistakes are prompted by both aspects of his idealism: his moral nobility, which leads him to spare and trust Antony for humanitarian reasons, and his tendency to let ideas obscure the complexity of the real world. His too simple analysis of the practical situation is typical of a theoretical thinker. He assumes that all men are like himself, that his colleagues' motives are as honourable as his own, that the Roman crowd can be permanently convinced by reason, that Antony will respect the spirit of the conditions he lays down for him to speak at Caesar's funeral; Cassius recognises the danger of this single-minded nobility:

> Therefore 'tis meet
> That noble minds keep ever with their likes. (I.ii.312–13)

Brutus's failure to plan any course of action to follow the assassination shows that he thinks that the majority of Romans are as devoted to the idea of the republic as he is himself, and that once Caesar is removed the old constitution will be automatically revived; so Brutus misses the tide and Antony takes the initiative. As he entangles himself in subtle hypotheses to justify the murder of Caesar, the image he uses to describe the disturbance in his mind – 'Like a phantasma, or a hideous dream' (II.i.65) – suggests he is leaving the world of reality for one of illusion, and it is ominous that his decision is clinched by deceit, not by the genuine appeals of honest Romans but by Cassius's fabricated letters (see p. 19).

3.4 THE PUBLIC FIGURE AND THE PRIVATE INDIVIDUAL

Brutus accepts Cassius's letters so readily because they chime in with his own image of himself as the hereditary champion of Roman liberty:

> My ancestors did from the streets of Rome
> The Tarquin drive, when he was called a king (II.i.53–4)

- but that was nearly five hundred years earlier. In his earlier approach to Brutus Cassius offers to be his 'glass' (I.ii.68) so that he can work on this image (I.ii.56-62, 159-61), as Decius exploits Caesar's self-image in order to deceive him (II.i.202-11; ii.83-9). For Brutus, like Caesar, suffers from a cult of personality: 'it sufficeth,' says Ligarius, 'That Brutus leads me on' (ii.i.333-4), and Brutus himself expects his reputation to be enough to satisfy the crowd of the truth of his assertions: 'Believe me for mine honour' (III.ii.14-15). The public images of both Brutus and Caesar have a firm basis in reality, but both men deceive themselves, and are deceived by others, when they come to accept the images as the whole truth about themselves - Caesar by insisting on his invulnerability, Brutus by the self-conscious assumption of moral and intellectual superiority that leads him to underestimate Antony and overbear Cassius with such effortless condescension. It was for his public image, as a figurehead, that the conspirators wanted Brutus; their tragedy, and perhaps it served them right, is that they got him as a leader.

The tragedy of Brutus is the more poignant in that to fulfil his public role, as he sees it, he has to sacrifice his personal affection for Caesar. In this he is the antithesis of Antony, for whom personal loyalty is paramount: whatever his faults, one cannot doubt the genuineness of Antony's love for Caesar or his contempt for the 'reasons' by which Brutus justifies the betrayal of his. One cannot blame Brutus for putting public responsibility above private affections although by killing Caesar he succeeds only in releasing the spirit of Caesarism in a more terrible form, in the debased tyranny of the Triumvirs, unrestrained by the relatively moderating influence of Caesar. As they coldly proscribe their enemies one might recall the generosity of the historical Caesar to his opponents, including Brutus (see p. 4); as Brutus himself says,

> I have not known when his affections swayed
> More than his reason. (II.i.20-1)

The tragedy is the greater in that it is in his personal relationships that Brutus can be admired with least qualification: in the mutual love and respect between him and Portia, his kindliness to his attendants, the warmth of friendship that finally breaks through his quarrel with Cassius. All this must be sacrificed along with his love of Caesar, but Brutus never suggests that the cost of public duty has been too high. His resolution in adversity is as admirable as the 'constancy' with which he goes through with the assassination. Yet this devotion to duty also gives rise to an inflexibility that prevents him from being one of Shakespeare's most sympathetic tragic heroes. He is burdened with regret at the necessity of killing Caesar and the failure of their cause, but he never shows any doubt about its morality, and all his accumulating errors fail to persuade him to doubt his own judgement. In Shakespeare's greatest tragedies, by the end of the play the hero has learnt from his suffering. But Brutus has learnt nothing; his self-image is still intact. While the audience is pitying his failure, he refuses to admit it. At his death he is still asserting his superiority over his enemies and claiming to gain more glory in defeat than they will by their 'vile conquest'. Yet his only certain achievement is in the sphere of personal relationships –

> My heart doth joy that yet in all my life
> I found no man but he was true to me (V.v.34–5)

– and in this celebration of loyalty, as Sir Mark Hunter comments, we are not intended to remember at this point in the play 'that of these true friends Caesar was one'.

4 DRAMATIC TECHNIQUES

4.1 SHAKESPEARE'S USE OF HIS SOURCE

No other of Shakespeare's major plays owes so much to its source as
Julius Caesar does to Plutarch's *Lives* (see p. 3). Not only are the characters developed from the brief studies Plutarch gives of the leading figures,
but the *Lives* also provided much of the dramatic background for the
events they record, such as the portents preceding the murder of Caesar,
and more personal episodes such as the quarrel between Brutus and
Cassius and Portia's appeal to Brutus. In Plutarch's account one can
already hear the elevated tone of Shakespeare's Brutus:

> lifting up his hands to heaven, he besought the gods to give him grace he
> might bring this episode to so good a pass, that he mgiht be found a
> husband worthy of so noble a wife as Porcia. (compare II.i.302-3)

Even in scenes for which Plutarch gave no detailed guidance Shakespeare
enters into the spirit of his account; the commentary on Brutus's speech
in the forum has already indicated how faithfully he interpreted Plutarch's
general description of his style (see p. 38). But it is Shakespeare who
recognises the dramatic potential and develops it by his selection and
ordering of the material, even when he follows Plutarch most closely.
Thus, finding in the *Lives* Caesar's comment on - according to Plutarch -
both Brutus and Cassius,

> As for those fat men and smooth-combed heads . . . I never reckon
> of them; but these pale-visaged and carrion-lean people, I fear them
> most,

he not only tightens the wording to form one of his most memorable
statements (I.ii.192-5), but expands on it to give a telling portrait of
Cassius, places it in the middle of Cassius's attack on Caesar so that each

provides a comment on the other, and uses it to give penetrating vignettes of Caesar and Antony in the interchange that follows.

4.2 STRUCTURE

Shakespeare's most obvious modification of Plutarch's account was to simplify and telescope the historical events. He combines Caesar's triumph of October 45BC with the Lupercal of the following February (see p. 6) and manipulates our sense of time so that the following scene (I.iii) seems to follow immediately from the Lupercal but ends on the morning of the ides of March (see p. 16). His dramatic sleight of hand is the more impressive in that he continually reminds us of the date and time as he exploits the drama in the Soothsayer's warning by detailing the approach of the fatal moment (II.i.40, 59, 213; ii.114; iv.23). After Caesar's murder the time scale is compressed more radically. The extended political manoeuvres that followed the assassination are compressed into the single dramatic confrontation between Antony and the conspirators. Eighteen months elapsed before the meeting of the Triumvirs depicted in IV.i and another year before the battle of Philippi, which was in fact two battles separated by twenty days; but while the audience must be vaguely aware of the passage of time for the opposing sides to gather their forces, the second half of the play gives the impression of fairly continuous action – particularly on the Elizabethan open stage where there was only a minimum of properties to indicate scene divisions.

This prevents any possibility of anti-climax after the assassination. We are swept immediately into the counter-action by the entry of Antony followed by his speech in the forum, which is as gripping as the murder itself; and then through two brief but highly dramatic scenes to the quarrel between Brutus and Cassius, with its new insights into their characters to increase the audience's sympathy before their deaths. Moreoever, the murder of Caesar has not removed him from the play. He dominates Antony's meeting with the conspirators and the speeches in the forum, with his bloodstained body as the physical focus of both episodes; he is a central issue in the quarrel between Brutus and Cassius as well as in the verbal hostilities between the rival leaders, and the actual appearance of his ghost to Brutus symbolises the way in which his spirit oppresses both him and Cassius as they approach defeat, both of them dying with the name of Caesar on their lips.

The concentration of the action is increased by the interlocking of scenes. The political discord presented in the first two scenes is followed by the symbolic storm, which then forms a background to the discord in Brutus's mind. The portents described by Casca and Calpurnia, and later by Cassius (V.i.80-9), with the prophetic dream of Calpurnia and the prophetic curse of Antony (III.i.259-75), and the appearance of Caesar's ghost, give a powerful sense of inevitability to the action, even though the outcome of the conspiracy is not pre-determined. There is a close parallelism between several of the scenes. The two night scenes, in Brutus's orchard and in his tent, are complementary (see p. 73); the scene between Caesar and Calpurnia follows that between Brutus and Portia; the hot-blooded murder of Cinna is followed by the cold-blooded planning of murder by the Triumvirs, and the covert plotting of Antony against Lepidus by the open quarrel between Brutus and Cassius. Parallel scenes are sharply juxtaposed to provide an implicit comment on each other.

4.3 CHARACTERISATION

The juxtapositioning of these scenes emphasies the pattern of contrasting characters in the play, centred on Brutus. In the first half his noble, but naive, disinterestedness is contrasted with Cassius's egotism and cunning; but in the second half Cassius's role as foil, or contrast, to Brutus is shared with Antony, and he can be viewed more sympathetically as the generous warmth of his relationship with Brutus contrasts with the calculating meanness of that between the Triumvirs.

The problems of the play are increased by the contrasting, even apparently contradictory, characteristics within individual characters. This often arises from the conflict between the public image that each maintains and the human being behind it: the character of **Caesar** is built up by the continual contrasting of public image with human failings. Too much is sometimes made of the latter. His superstition may be a failing, but he is only adopting traditional beliefs (I.ii.7-9), which even Cassius finally comes to accept (V.i.77-89) – in fact, it would have been better for Caesar had he been more, not less, superstitious. His physical weaknesses do not in themselves diminish his greatness, but only by showing up the absurdity of his claims to be more than human. But this arrogance is only greatness going to seed; the public image is not all show. Sometimes, in fact, it is difficult to distinguish the genuine from the false: is Caesar's refusal to read Artemidorus's petition (III.i.8) true magnanimity or merely a gesture to please the crowd? Once he is dead his human weaknesses die with him and we are left only with the genuine greatness vividly recalled by Antony – and not only by him. It is often said that Caesar's reputation enabled Shakespeare to emphasise his failings because he could take his heroic stature for granted, and it is striking that some of the most impressive tributes to his pre-eminence come from the men who murdered him. To Brutus he is still 'the foremost man of all this world' (IV.iii.22) and it is Cassius at his most virulent who provides the image that sums up his supremacy:

> Why man, he doth bestride the narrow world
> Like a Colossus. (I.ii.135-6)

As Antony says of his own praise of Caesar,

> The enemies of Caesar shall say this;
> Then, in a friend, it is cold modesty. (III.i.212-13)

Brutus's character is also developed by our seeing him as both the public figure and a private individual, but while Caesar retains his public manner even when talking to his wife, Brutus's domestic life reveals the humanity that lies behind the public persona. We see more deeply into Brutus than into Caesar, and Shakespeare presents a consistent portrait of a Stoic (see p. 52), with both the Stoic's virtues and his faults – the high principles and sense of duty, but also the moral arrogance and the austerity that can seem like coldness. Nobility and self-restraint are ingrained in his character. It is to this fundamental coherence that Antony pays tribute:

> and the elements
> So mixed in him that Nature might stand up
> And say to all the world, 'This was a man'. (V.v.73-5)

It is reflected in the harmony of music, to which Brutus naturally turns even on the eve of battle, and the contrast between his normal equanimity and the less stable, fiery Cassius is pointed by Caesar's comment that the latter 'hears no music' (I.ii.204). But this inner harmony is fully experienced only in such moments when Brutus can escape from his public responsibilities. At the beginning of the play his equilibrium has already been disturbed by his inner conflict, and his subsequent moral assertiveness and self-contradictions result from his effort to preserve his integrity while torn by conflicting loyalties.

In contrast to Brutus's Antony's public image is one of frivolous irresponsibility, and his sudden transformation into a serious political force is a master-stroke of dramatic surprise. It is carefully prepared, for there is no inconsistency between the 'gamesome' Antony and the skilful demagogue who emerges after the assassination. As the critic John Palmer has pointed out, it is because he is given to 'much company' (II.i.189) that he can establish such a rapport with the crowd, and he plays the game of politics with the mixture of recklessness and finesse of a born sportsman. The depth of his love for Caesar may be surprising, but Cassius already feared it (II.i.184), and the old irresponsibility is still there as he releases the destructive forces he has aroused (II.ii. 269-70) and plots to cheat the citizens of Caesar's bequests and to outmanoeuvre Lepidus (IV.i.8-9. 12-27).

The contrasting attributes of some of the other characters are less easily resolved. So great is the difference between Casca's sycophantic attitude when we first meet him (I.ii.1, 14) and his contemptuous account of Caesar's refusal of the crown, and between this cynical realism and his superstitious fear in the storm, that it has been suggested that Shakespeare added his description of the scene in the forum at a late stage in the composition of the play and then gave Casca his distinctively 'sour' manner. But so radical an explanation is not necessary. The one thing that Shakespeare knew about Casca is that he struck the first blow at Caesar from behind. This comes to symbolise the treachery of the conspiracy (V.i.41-4), so it is entirely appropriate that he should flatter Caesar to his face and then stab him verbally in the back. Moreover, his manner is so self-consciously surly that it is clearly a pose; it is a sign of weakness, not strength, so it is not surprising that his self-confidence should be shattered by the storm. It is yet another example of a public manner being cultivated to conceal inner failings.

Cassius presents a more challenging problem. In the first half of the play he might seem merely the scheming politician, motivated by personal envy, prepared to deceive Brutus and congratulating himself sardonically on his success (I.ii.310-24), yet by the end he has revealed an intense love of Brutus and is even described as the embodiment of Roman virtues, 'The last of all the Romans' (V.iii.99). Yet Cassius is very much of a piece. He is more sympathetic in the second half of the play because we come to know him more intimately: he inherited his 'rash humour' from his mother (IV.iii.120), it is his birthday, and we are admitted into his confidence by his quiet word aside to Messala (V.i.71-6). This more sympathetic presentation prepares us for the tributes at his death, but, as Antony says, he is 'Old Cassius still' (V.i.63), casual about moral issues and prone to angry outbursts. For all his shrewd calculation he is very emotional, liable to swing between extremes as he does between anger and grief in his quarrel with Brutus, and given to dramatic gestures (I.iii.46-52, 111-15; III.i.20-2, 80-1; IV.iii.100-7). It is in character that his suicide - his last dramatic gesture, this time for real - should be prompted by the capture of his best friend (V.iii.34-5), for Cassius sees everything in personal terms. As his enmity to Caesar stems from personal envy, so his quarrel with Brutus is precipitated by a personal affront - his letters have been slighted (IV.iii.4-5) - and it is the loss of Brutus's friendship that overwhelms him. His distress may be surprising in its intensity, but some indication of his dependence on Brutus has already been given by the way he turns to him when he thinks they have been betrayed (III.i.20). His passionate lament that concludes the quarrel seems far removed from his cynical reflections on his manipulation of Brutus at the end of I.ii., but they have one thing in common: a bitter comment on the love between Brutus and Caesar and his own exclusion from it (I.ii.315-17; IV.iii.105-7). The tone of violent jealousy at the end of the quarrel is unmistakeable, and suggests that the cynicism with which he had previously contemplated his success in wooing Brutus away from Caesar reflects the spite of a jealous lover as well as the self-satisfaction of a scheming politician. The concern that Cassius expresses on his first approach to Brutus that he is not receiving the 'show of love' from him that he 'was wont to have' (I.ii.34) may be more genuinely felt than might at first appear.

There are, however, other possible interpretations of Cassius's soliloquy at the end of I.ii (see pp. 13-14), and one reason why there can be such diverse reactions to the characters in *Julius Caesar* is that there are comparatively few soliloquies in which they reveal their inner thoughts unambiguously to the audience. In Brutus's soliloquy in his orchard (II.i.10-34), for example, he is reasoning with himself to justify the murder of Caesar rather than expressing his feelings. It is rare for a character to speak directly from the heart, as Brutus does when he describes his mental turmoil (II.i.61-9) or Antony when he is alone with Caesar's corpse (III.i.254-75). More characteristic of the play is the way in which the characters view themselves from the outside, as they do when they refer to themselves in the third person (see p. 8). Caesar, of course, constantly identifies himself with the heroic figure of 'Caesar' that he wants the Romans to see, and other characters also adopt this practice when they are presenting an ideal image of themselves, the qualities to be expected of a Brutus (I.ii.172-5; II.i. 56-8; IV.iii.79-82; V.i.111-13), a Cassius (I.iii.90; III.i.20-2; IV.iii.93-5), even a Casca (I.iii.116-17). This self-consciousness is not necessarily egotistical; often it is the means by which a character holds up to himself the code of conduct by which he strives to live, or sometimes has it held up to him. Thus Brutus rebukes Cassius with his name – 'The name of Cassius honours this corruption' (IV.iii.15) – and Cassius ironically contrasts Brutus's name with that of Caesar to incite Brutus to live up to the responsibilities inherited with his name (i.ii.142-61; see p. 11). But the name that is most insistent throughout the play is that of Rome itself. The word 'Roman' is enough to invoke those qualities of civic responsibility, honour and fortitude that all the characters claim to uphold. It is this that gives both the play and its characters their impressive and moving nobility.

4.4 STYLE AND IMAGERY

It has been said that this common 'Roman' quality and the rhetorical style of speech obscure the differences between the characters. *Julius Caesar* is certainly more concerned with the relation of individuals to political events than with intimate self-revelation. The characters are constantly occupied in persuading others, even in the more domestic scenes, and the speeches are subtly and elaborately constructed, using all the arts of rhetoric that are illustrated in the detailed analysis of Brutus's speech to the crowd (pp.38-9) and in the critical analysis (pp. 75-7), as well as more generally throughout the commentary. But 'rhetorical' should not be understood in its popular sense of 'artificial', as in 'mere rhetoric'; it can be that, but Portia's appeal to Brutus is equally rhetorical in its quiet, persuasive irony and finely controlled climaxes. The rhetoric differs widely in style, and distinguishes rather than obscures the personalities of the speakers. In their speeches in the forum Brutus's terse prose could not be more different from Antony's supple, emotional blank verse; and while Cassius's speeches in I.ii are as passionate as those of Antony, his forthright bitterness is totally different from Antony's insinuating irony.

The structure of the speeches may be complex, but the vocabulary is generally simple. The most memorable lines have an unadorned clarity and strength: 'Cowards die many times before their deaths . . .' (II.ii.32); 'There is a tide in the affairs of men . . .' (IV.iii.218); 'The fault, dear Brutus, is not in our stars, But in ourselves . . .' (I.ii.140-1). The style of the play as a whole reflects the nobility and austerity that is associated with the highest Roman ideals.

The directness and simplicity of the imagery has a similar Roman strength. A recurrent theme is the working of metals (I.ii.311; II.i.61, 210; III.i.175; V.iii. 75-8) - with a neat pun on 'metal' and 'mettle' (I.i.63; ii.298, 311; II.i.134) - which is linked with the use of steel to strike a spark from flint (I.ii.176-7; II.i.120-1; IV.iii.111-13) to suggest the fortitude and spiritedness of a Roman: 'those sparks of life That should be in a Roman' (I.iii.57-8). This, in turn, links the metallic imagery to the metaphorical references to fire (I.ii.186; iii.107-8, 130; II.i.332; III.i.37, 171; ii.119) that culminate in the literal burning of the conspirators' houses and Portia's suicide by swallowing fire. This interrelation of the imagery gives imaginative cohesion to the play and comments unobtrusively on the action, as, for example, Brutus's wish that they should not hew Caesar 'as a carcass fit for hounds' (II.i.174) is countered by Antony's presentation of them as blood-stained hunters dividing the 'spoil' so that he can himself 'let slip the dogs of war' (III.i.204-6, 273).

The imagery of light and darkness provides a similar symbolic comment. It is ominous that the conspirators meet at night to plan both the assassination and their military strategy. Darkness is explicitly related to the deceitfulness of conspiracy (II.i.77-9) and with disease and the 'sick offence' in Brutus's mind (II.i.261-8). Lucius, whose name means 'light', brings a brief gleam of illumination into the darkness (II.i.35; IV.iii.157), as the clear assurance of Brutus's domestic life shines through the obscurity of his involvement in political affairs. His restlessness is twice contrasted with Lucius's innocent slumber (II.i.229-33; IV.iii.267-70), and he compares his state of mind to 'a phantasma, or a hideous dream' (II.i.65) - a phantasma that finally manifests itself in the 'monstrous apparition' of Caesar's ghost (IV.iii.277), which is itself a materialisation of the many references to Caesar's spirit. The conspirators look to the new dawn of republican liberty (II.i.105-11), but at the end of the play the encroaching darkness is emphasised: 'The deep of night is crept upon our talk' (IV.iii.226). Brutus is satisfied merely 'that the day will end' (V.ii.125) and while Cassius's death is irradiated by the setting sun - 'The sun of Rome is set' (V.iii.60-4) - he resigns himself to darkness: 'Night hangs upon mine eyes; my bones would rest' (V.v.41). Poetic metaphor constantly interacts with the actual setting and events of the play, and the portents are visible and audible symbols of the coming civil strife. Blood and fire predominate in them: as Cassius says,

> the complexion of the element
> In favour's like the work we have in hand,
> Most bloody, fiery, and most terrible. (I.iii.128-30)

The play is full of images of blood. Roman virtues are identified with Roman blood: Caesar has triumphed over 'Pompey's blood' (I.i.53), Rome has 'lost the breed of noble bloods' (I.ii.151), the conspirators' blood would be guilty of bastardy if they broke their word (II.i.136-40), and Caesar's blood – 'the most noble blood of all this world' (III.i.156) – would be 'rebel blood' if he gave way to flattery (III.i.40). Antony continually reminds us of Caesar's blood, both on his corpse and on the murderers. To develop its symbolism Shakespeare makes his most significant changes to his source. According to Plutarch, Calpurnia's dream was that a pinnacle on Caesar's house had been broken down; Shakespeare's alteration of this to Caesar's statue spouting blood was probably suggested by the statement in North's translation of the *Lives* that during the assassination Pompey's statue 'ran all of a gore blood', which was itself a misunderstanding of Plutarch's statement that the base of the statue was drenched with blood. Ironically, both Calpurnia and Decius are correct in their interpretations of the dream: Caesar is murdered, but his blood is 'Reviving blood' (II.ii.88), although not as the sacrificial blood that Brutus intended to revive the republic, but as Antony uses it to revive the spirit of Caesarism. Plutarch records that the conspirators wounded each other accidentally in the press round Caesar; Shakespeare changes this to the conspirators' bathing their hands in Caesar's blood, a ritual that was intended to show the sacrificial nature of the murder, but which Antony seizes on to emphasise its brutality. The conflict between Brutus's unrealistic idealism and Antony's opportunist realism is summed up by these rival interpretations: Caesar's blood is the symbolic focus of the play.

5 SPECIMEN CRITICAL ANALYSIS

MARULLUS Wherefore rejoice? What conquest brings he home?
What tributaries follow him to Rome,
To grace in captive bonds his chariot-wheels?
You blocks, you stones, you worse than senseless things!
O you hard hearts, you cruel men of Rome,
Knew you not Pompey? Many a time and oft
Have you climbed up to walls and battlements,⠀⠀⠀⠀⠀⠀40
To towers and windows, yea, to chimney-tops,
Your infants in your arms, and there have sat
The livelong day, with patient expectation,
To see great Pompey pass the streets of Rome;
And when you saw his chariot but appear,
Have you not made an universal shout,
That Tiber trembled underneath her banks
To hear the replication of your sounds
Made in her concave shores?
And do you now put on your best attire?⠀⠀⠀⠀⠀⠀50
And do you now cull out a holiday?
And do you now strew flowers in his way
That comes in triumph over Pompey's blood?
Be gone!
Run to your houses, fall upon your knees,
Pray to the gods to intermit the plague
That needs must light on this ingratitude. (I.i.34–57)

Marullus is rebuking a group of commoners for going to acclaim Caesar in the triumphal procession to celebrate his victory over Pompey's sons. The eloquence of his blank verse is in marked contrast to the commoners' colloquial prose that precedes it, as the intensity of his rebuke contrasts with their casual readiness to cheer anyone who is the current hero. Marullus's outraged feelings are conveyed by rhetorical forms, with subtle changes of pace and emphasis, rather than by figurative language. It sounds like a natural outburst, but it is very precisely structured. The central extended description, recalling how the crowd had welcomed Pompey back to Rome (39-49), is framed between two sections with a much tighter structure, based on a repeated threefold pattern: at the start three rhetorical questions (34-6) followed by three terms of abuse (37), and at the end three more rhetorical questions (50-3) followed by three commands (55-7). (Rhetorical questions are questions that do not require an answer and are merely a method of emphasising the statements they imply, either because they are simply statements given an interrogative form (50-3), or because only one answer is possible (34-6).) In each trio, moreover, the third element is longer than the others, giving the effect of a subsidiary climax.

The Second Citizen's cheerful banter is abruptly cut short when Marullus picks up the word 'rejoice' and flings it back at him, 'Wherefore rejoice?', and the two rhetorical questions that follow emphasise how unworthy Caesar's victory is of a triumph. It is fellow Romans he has defeated; he has made no foreign conquests, nor brought back captive chieftains to pay tribute money to Rome. At the same time they suggest the magnificence of a genuine Roman triumph. The movement is dignified and the language ceremonial; the brutality of dragging fettered captives behind a chariot is glossed over; the tributaries 'follow' the conqueror to Rome and 'grace' his chariot wheels; even iron fetters are softened to 'captive bonds'.

The mood changes from lofty indignation to blunt abuse as Marullus rounds on his listeners, 'You blocks, you stones'; the phrases expand to a climax, 'you worse than senseless things' – they are not merely unfeeling, like stones, but corrupted in their feelings – and then levels off in the evenly balanced 'O you hard hearts, you cruel men of Rome'. The line moves very deliberately; the rebuke is still powerful, with the accent falling on the equally stressed 'hard hearts' and the word 'cruel' prolonged by the metre, but the tone has changed from the hard anger of the previous line to a more impassioned lament, in preparation for the reference to Pompey. So far Marullus has held back the point of his rebuke; his startled audience must be at a loss to know how they have caused this outburst, and now he springs it on them, 'Knew you not Pompey?' The implication must be obvious: they cannot have forgotten their former hero, and it is a victory over Pompey's sons that they are thoughtlessly going to celebrate.

There is a brief pause after that potent name before Marullus drives his point home by reminding them with vivid detail of their former adulation of Caesar's defeated enemy. Now the movement of the verse is more expansive and the phrasing fuller, recalling former times with the leisurely 'Many a time and oft'. Matching the action described, the rhythm climbs steadily through the sequence, 'to walls and battlements, To towers and windows, yea, to chimney-tops' – another trio of phrases, with the climax of the ascent lightly marked by the momentary lingering on 'yea' – 'yes, even'. But there is no interruption to the smooth progression as the verse moves to its stately climax, 'To see great Pompey pass the streets of Rome'. Here there is a more marked pause before the movement is picked up again, through the mounting excitement of 'And when you saw his chariot but appear' to their 'universal shout', which is held reverberating through the next three lines. The effect is to give a very flattering impression of the crowd. The dignified progress of Pompey 'passing' the streets of Rome is matched by their controlled ascent to the chimney-tops; they are all good family men – 'Your infants in your arms' – and they sit 'with patient expectation': this is an orderly, disciplined crowd. And as the greatness of Pompey is linked with the greatness of Rome, so they are reminded of their own status as Roman citizens. Even in his earlier abuse Marullus addressed them as 'men of Rome', and their unity with each other and with their city is given concrete expression by their 'universal' shout; it fills the city, echoing between the banks of the Tiber – the river of Rome – its reverberation felt as physical vibrations as 'Tiber trembled underneath her banks'. This elaborate metaphor – almost the only one in the speech – with the personification of the river suggesting its special significance to the Romans, elevates their communal shout into an impressive symbol of civic unity.

After this fluent description the curtness of the next trio of rhetorical questions conveys Marullus's contempt for the present festivities, and is reinforced by the scornful repetition of 'And do you now', although the repetition gives even scorn a certain formality. The ceremonial dignity of Pompey's triumphs is trivialised to a 'holiday'. The final defeat of their former hero's cause is regarded merely as an opportunity for their own enjoyment; 'cull' is generally used of picking flowers and anticipates the strewing of flowers before the man who has triumphed over 'Pompey's blood'. The verse structure is disrupted to give authority to the curt order, 'Be gone!', and then the rhetorical pattern is restored by Marullus's three urgent commands instructing them to hasten to appease the gods and escape divine retribution.

While Marullus castigates the fickleness of the commoners, he also presents an idealised portrait of them at their best against which to measure their deterioration through the next three acts as they are manipulated by other skilful orators. At the same time this speech provides a condensed image of Rome – the greatness of its victories, its triumphs, its military heroes and teeming commoners, its streets, its buildings (even if the details suggest Elizabethan London rather than classical Rome), its river and its gods. It outlines at the beginning of the play the political situation that is the source of the ensuing tragedy, and conveys a sense of the civic pride and respect for Roman tradition that animates the actors in it.

6 CRITICAL APPROACHES

Julius Caesar has always been a popular play, although it has sometimes tended to arouse more admiration than enthusiasm. Even in the eighteenth century, when its rhetorical style and classical restraint were most likely to be appreciated, Dr Johnson found it 'somewhat cold and unaffecting': Shakespeare's 'adherence to the real story, and to *Roman* manners, seems to have impeded the natural vigour of his genius'. Johnson acknowledged, however, that the Quarrel Scene 'is universally celebrated', and the special appeal of that scene to early audiences is evident from Leonard Digges's commendatory verses to Shakespeare's *Poems* (1640), in which he singles it out for special mention:

> So have I seene, when Cesar would appeare,
> And on the Stage at halfe-sword Parley were,
> *Brutus* and *Cassius*: oh how the Audience,
> Were ravish'd, with what wonder they went thence.

More recently Mark Van Doren has complained that the play has 'more rhetoric than poetry' –

its persons all have something of the statue in them, for they express their author's idea of antiquity rather than his knowledge of life'
(*Shakespeare*, 1939)

– but the tendency of most twentieth-century critical studies has been to challenge this impression of 'remote Roman grandeur'. In *The Imperial Theme* (1931) Wilson Knight emphasised the emotional intensity of the play, seeing its theme as the opposition of love, which is creative of order, and honour, to which Brutus always sacrifices love. His characteristically symbolic interpretation largely ignores the political structure of the play – 'Cassius and Antony are both order-forces, love-forces in the play' – but he makes a stimulating case for Cassius, who is 'always in touch with realities – of love, of conspiracy, of war', while 'Brutus is ever more at home with ethical abstractions'. L. C. Knights pursues a somewhat similar theme more circumspectly in *Further Explorations* (1965). In politics

the issues are to some extent simplified and generalised, and therefore seen in abstract and schematic terms. Morality . . . has to do with the human, the specific and particular.

When Brutus decides that Caesar must be killed (II.i.10–34) he dismisses what he knows of him personally as irrelevant to public considerations, so that '*what is* is . . . completely lost in a cloud of mere possibilities', and Brutus is delivered 'to a world of unreality', a 'phantasmagoria of abstractions'. One such abstraction is Brutus's interpretation of the ritual bathing of the conspirators' hands in Caesar's blood, and Leo Kirschbaum, in 'Shakespeare's Stage Blood' (*Publications of the Modern Language Society of America*, LXIV, 1949), points out how critics and producers have evaded the 'shocking gory effect' of this. But by adding this ritual to Plutarch's narrative Shakespeare intended to shock: 'All murder is in the act savage and inhuman, Shakespeare is saying'.

Julius Caesar seems austere not because the characters are unemotional but rather because it does not have the uniquely dense imaginative texture of Shakespeare's other major tragedies. But this is only relative: the symbolic power of the key images (see pp. 73–4) is now recognised, and studies such as R. A. Foakes's 'An Approach to *Julius Caesar*' (*Shakespeare Quarterly*, V, 1954) have shown how sequences of related images give imaginative substance to the play's themes. Thus Brutus pretends sickness to Portia, but finds his sickness is real – he has a 'sick offence' within his mind (II.i.268) – and instead of making 'sick men whole' (II.i.327) the assassination only extends the sickness: the love between Cassius and Brutus 'begins to sicken and decay' (IV.ii.20), Brutus is 'sick of many griefs' (IV.iii.144), and the carrion birds look down on them as if they 'were sickly prey' (V.i.87). From a detailed study of the language and imagery Foakes concludes that 'language and action all suggest a full circle of events . . . civil war leading to civil war, blood to blood'.

The reputation of Brutus, the idealist, has inevitably suffered from this emphasis on the emotional, physical and imaginative impact of the play. Earlier critics had been aware of the ambiguities in his character. Swinburne might regard him as the ideal republican, or Sir Mungo MacCallum as 'a patriotic gentleman of the best Roman or best English type (*Shakespeare's Roman Plays,* 1910), but Edward Dowden anticipated much subsequent criticism with his trenchant comment:

It is idealists who create a political terror; they are free from all desire of blood-shedding; but to them the lives of men and women are accidents; the lives of ideas are the true realities; and, armed with an abstract principle and a suspicion, they perform deeds which are at once beautiful and hideous. (*Shakspere: A Critical Study of His Mind and Art,* 1875)

In this century critics have made an increasingly close analysis of the characters and their motives, with particular attention to Brutus's now notorious soliloquy at the beginning of Act II. For Granville-Barker, Shakespeare's chief interest lay in 'the spiritual problem of the virtuous murderer ... Do evil that good may come, and see what does come!' (*Prefaces to Shakespeare*, 1930), but while he concedes that Brutus 'tries many of us as high as he tries Cassius' his chief criticism of his character is that Shakespeare fails to 'make' anything of him at the end of the play:

> when we expect ... some deeper revelation, some glimpse of the hero's very soul, this hero stays inarticulate, or, worse, turns oracular.

In the following year, however, Brutus's character was analysed incisively by Sir Mark Hunter, who concluded that 'Noble-hearted and sincere beyond question, he is intellectually dishonest' (*Royal Society of Literature: Essays by Divers Hands*, X, 1931). Caesar, on the other hand, 'moves before us as something right royal' – otherwise, Hunter argues, the tributes to him by Antony and Brutus will seem inconsistent with what we have seen and heard. Soon, though, the rise of European dictatorships put the play in a completely new perspective, exemplified by Dover Wilson's Introduction to the New Cambridge edition (1948), in which he describes Caesar as 'the universal dictator' and Caesarism as 'a secular threat to the human spirit'. He considers Brutus completely justified in fearing that power would change Caesar's character and that 'Shakespeare does all he can to show that the reading of Caesar's character in the soliloquy [II.i. 10–34] is correct'.

Between these extremes critics such as John Palmer have done more justice to the complexity of the play. Palmer's analysis of it in *Political Characters of Shakespeare* (1945) is full of insights into both its characters and its structure. Caesar binds the first and second parts together: 'He is exhibited from the outset as a man who will be mightier in death than in life'. His greatness is assumed throughout the play, and after his death we are taken into a 'diminished world ... in Rome which has lost her master', a diminution evident in the mean scheming of the Triumvirs and the childish wrangling of Brutus and Cassius. Yet it is Palmer who justifies the notorious line, 'Caesar did never wrong but with just cause' as 'Shakespeare's finishing touch to the portrait of a dictator' (see p. 32), although he too considers that Brutus suffers from the 'fundamental lie in his character',

> the lie that sooner or later is impressed on any idealist who enters public life and must use means which he despises to achieve ends which have no true bearing on the political realities about him.

What, then, is the unfortunate idealist to do; should Brutus have merely acquiesced in Caesar's dictatorship? The critic is tempted to remain sitting on the fence, and in *Shakespeare's Problem Plays* (1963) Ernest Schanzer made that posture intellectually respectable. He argues that there can be no final answer to the question since it depends on one's view of Caesar. We are given 'a series of images of Caesar', by Cassius, Casca, Brutus, Artemidorus and Antony, and while doubt is thrown on most of them, Shakespeare's own presentation of Caesar is so ambiguous that none is entirely dispelled. He seems to be asking, 'Which is the real Caesar?'; we may even feel that 'there *is* no real Caesar, that he merely exists as a set of images in other men's minds and his own'. While the conspiracy is clearly a catastrophe, Shakespeare does not 'make wholly clear its moral indefensibility', so that *Julius Caesar* is of its very nature a 'problem play'.

QUESTIONS

1. When Artemidorus presents his schedule, do you hope that Caesar will, or will not, read it? Consider why you react as you do.
2. Which character would you choose to act in the play and what aspects of the character would particularly interest you? Taking relevant episodes from the play, explain, or demonstrate, how you would convey these by speech and action.
3. 'The nature of the real Caesar remains an enigma' (Schanzer). How far do you think you can solve the enigma?
4. Brutus 'is so impossibly noble: and when we forget his nobility he becomes just "impossible" ' (Wilson Knight). Is this fair to Brutus?
5. T. S. Dorsch suggests that in agreeing that his nephew be put to death Antony might not be callous, but just and unsentimental: he shows he will not be swayed by family ties if Publius is a threat to them. How far can you defend Antony's conduct in the play?
6. 'All men's motives are mixed: Cassius hates Caesar, but that does not mean that all his talk of liberty and equality is insincere'. Do you agree?
7. How justified do you think Brutus's claim that he will have more glory by 'this losing day' than Octavius and Antony by their 'vile conquest'?
8. What would be lost if the women characters were omitted from the play?
9. 'Shakespeare was not a democrat, but he was not unsympathetic to the common people.' What is your impression of the crowd in the play?
10. After the assassination Cassius as well as Brutus addresses the crowd (III.ii.3–10). Write Cassius's speech.
11. How, as a producer, would you present Act III, scene i, lines 1–79, or a shorter extract including the assassination, in order to bring out what you think to be important in the episode?
12.   But men may construe things, after their fashion,
        Clean from the purpose of the things themselves.

In what ways does the play illustrate the truth of Cicero's comment?
13. What is the function in the play of superstition and the supernatural?
14.   Therefore 'tis meet
      That noble minds keep ever with their likes;
      For who so firm that cannot be seduced? (I.ii.312-14)
Does the play demonstrate that there is no place for idealism in politics?
15. Consider the treatment in the play of one of the following: friendship; loyalty; tyranny.
16. For the purpose of conveying the themes of the play, what would be the advantages and disadvantages of setting a production in (a) ancient Rome, (b) Elizabethan England, or (c) your own country in the second half of the twentieth-century.
17. What impression does the play give of the qualities implied by 'Roman'?
18. Make a close critical analysis of II.i.233-56 ('Brutus, my lord ... your case of grief') or I.iii. 3-32 ('Are you not moved ... that they point upon'), or examine the imagery in the second passage to show how it relates to the themes of the play.

APPENDIX :

SHAKESPEARE'S THEATRE

BY HAROLD BROOKS

We should speak, as Murel Bradbrook reminds us, not of the Elizabethan stage but of Elizabethan stages. Plays of Shakespeare were acted on tour, in the halls of mansions, one at least in Gray's Inn, frequently at Court, and after 1609 at the Blackfriars, a small, roofed theatre for those who could afford the price. But even after his Company acquired the Blackfriars, we know of no play of his not acted (unless, rather improbably, *Troilus* is an exception) for the general public at the Globe, or before 1599 at its predecessor, The Theatre, which, since the Globe was constructed from the same timbers, must have resembled it. Describing the Globe, we can claim therefore to be describing, in an acceptable sense, Shakespeare's theatre, the physical structure his plays were designed to fit. Even in the few probably written for a first performance elsewhere, adaptability to that structure would be in his mind.

For the facilities of the Globe we have evidence from the drawing of the Swan theatre (based on a sketch made by a visitor to London about 1596) which depicts the interior of another public theatre; the builder's contract for the Fortune theatre, which in certain respects (fortunately including the dimensions and position of the stage) was to copy the Globe; indications in the dramatic texts; comments, like Ben Jonson's on the throne let down from above by machinery; and eye-witness testimony to the number of spectators (in round figures, 3000) accommodated in the auditorium.

In communicating with the audience, the actor was most favourably placed. Soliloquising at the centre of the front of the great platform, he was at the mid-point of the theatre, with no one among the spectators more than sixty feet away from him. That platform-stage (Figs I and II) was the most important feature for performance at the Globe. It had the audience – standing in the yard (10) and seated in the galleries (9) – on three sides of it. It was 43 feet wide, and 27½ feet from front to back. Raised (?5½ feet) above the level of the yard, it had a trap-door (II.8) giving access to the space below it. The actors, with their equipment, occupied the 'tiring house' (attiring-house: 2) immediately at the back of the stage. The stage-direction 'within' means inside the tiring-house. Along its frontage, probably from the top of the second storey, juts out the canopy or 'Heavens', carried on two large pillars rising through the platform (6, 7) and sheltering the rear part of the stage, the rest of which, like the yard, was open to the sky. If the 'hut' (I.8), housing the machinery for descents, stood, as in the Swan drawing, above the 'Heavens', that covering must have had a trap-door, so that the descents could be made through it.

Descents are one illustration of the vertical dimension the dramatist could use to supplement the playing-area of the great platform. The other opportunities are provided by the tiring-house frontage or facade. About this facade the evidence is not as complete or clear as we should like, so that Fig. I is in part conjectural. Two doors giving entry to the platform there certainly were (3). A third (4) is probable but not certain. When curtained, a door, most probably this one, would furnish what must be termed a discovery-space (II.5), not an inner stage (on which action in any depth would have been out of sight for a significant part of the audience). Usually no more than two actors were revealed (exceptionally, three), who often then moved out on to the platform. An example of this is Ferdinand and Miranda in *The Tempest* 'discovered' at chess, then seen on the platform speaking with their fathers. Similarly the gallery (I.5) was not an upper stage. Its use was not limited to the actors: sometimes it functioned as 'lords' rooms' for favoured spectators, sometimes, perhaps, as a musicians' gallery. Frequently the whole gallery would not be needed for what took place aloft: a window-stage (as in the first balcony scene in *Romeo*, even perhaps in the second) would suffice. Most probably this would be a part (at one end) of the gallery itself; or just possibly, if the gallery did not (as it does in the Swan drawing) extend the whole width of the tiring-house, a window over the left or right-hand door. As the texts show, whatever was presented aloft, or in the discovery-space, was directly related to the action on the platform, so that at no time was there left, between the audience and the action of the drama, a great bare space of platform-stage. In relating Shakespeare's drama to the physical conditions of the theatre, the primacy of that platform is never to be forgotten.

Note: The present brief account owes most to C. Walter Hodges, *The Globe Restored*; Richard Hosley in *A New Companion to Shakespeare Studies*, and in *The Revels History of English Drama*; and to articles by Hosley and Richard Southern in *Shakespeare Survey*, 12, 1959, where full discussion can be found.

HAROLD BROOKS

SHAKESPEARE'S THEATRE

The stage and its adjuncts; the tiring-house; and the auditorium.

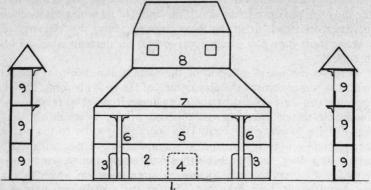

FIG I ELEVATION

1. Platform stage (approximately five feet above the ground) 2. Tiring-house
3. Tiring-house doors to stage 4. Conjectural third door 5. Tiring-house
gallery (balustrade and partitioning not shown) 6. Pillars supporting the
heavens 7. The heavens 8. The hut 9. The spectators' galleries

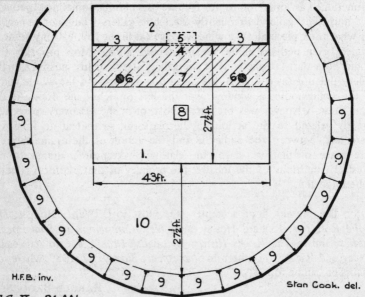

FIG II PLAN

1. Platform stage 2. Tiring-house 3. Tiring-house doors to stage
4. Conjectural third door 5. Conjectural discovery space (alternatively behind 3)
6. Pillars supporting the heavens 7. The heavens 8. Trap door 9. Spectators'
gallery 10. The yard

The Globe

An artist's imaginative recreation of a typical Elizabethan theatre

FURTHER READING

Collections of Extracts from Important Critical Works
Dean, L. (ed.), *Twentieth Century Interpretations of Julius Caesar* (Prentice Hall, 1977)
Ure, P. (ed.), *Julius Caesar, a Casebook* (Macmillan, 1969)

Critical Works Containing Substantial Sections on Julius Caesar
Bonjour, A., *The Structure of Julius Caesar* (Liverpool University Press, 1958)
Foakes, B. A., 'An Approach to *Julius Caesar*', in *Shakespeare Quarterly*, V (1954)
Granville-Barker, H., *Prefaces to Shakespeare, First Series* (1930; paperback, Batsford, 1963)
Hunter, M., 'Politics and Character in Shakespeare's *Julius Caesar*', in *Royal Society of Literature Essays by Divers Hands*, X, 1931)
Knight, G. Wilson, *The Imperial Theme* (Methuen, 1931, revised edn 1951)
Knights, L. C., *Further Explorations* (Chatto, 1965)
MacCallum, M. W., *Shakespeare's Roman Plays and their Background* (Macmillan, 1910, 1964)
Palmer, J., *Political Characters of Shakespeare* (Macmillan, 1945)
Schanzer, E., *Shakespeare's Problem Plays* (Routledge, 1963)
Stewart, J. I. M., *Character and Motive in Shakespeare* (Longmans, 1949)
Van Doren, M., *Shakespeare* (Henry Holt, 1939)

The Source of the Play
Spenser, T. J. B., *Shakespeare's Plutarch* (Penguin, 1964)

The Sussex Tape of *Julius Caesar* (Educational Productions Ltd) includes a discussion of general issues in the play and recorded scenes which are discussed by the actors.